T0128285

# LIFE IS HARD...
## Choose Jesus

devotions of intentional faith

Pam Lynch Williams

WESTBOW
P R E S S®
A DIVISION OF THOMAS NELSON
& ZONDERVAN

WestBow Press books may be ordered through booksellers or by contacting:

WestBow Press
A Division of Thomas Nelson & Zondervan
1663 Liberty Drive
Bloomington, IN 47403
www.westbowpress.com
844-714-3454

Scripture quotations marked ESV are from the ESV Bible® (The Holy Bible, English Standard Version®), copyright © 2001 by Crossway Bibles, a publishing ministry of Good News Publishers. Used by permission. All rights reserved.

Scripture quotations marked KJV are taken from the Holy Bible, King James Version.

ISBN: 978-1-6642-9174-4 (sc)
ISBN: 978-1-6642-9175-1 (hc)
ISBN: 978-1-6642-9173-7 (e)

Library of Congress Control Number: 2023908256

Print information available on the last page.

WestBow Press rev. date:   07/19/2023

Our faith is a choice, a daily choice, to follow Jesus. Life is hard, and happiness is temporary. Jesus is the constant, and we have to choose to walk with Him day after day.

This book is a collection of daily devotions that weave in everyday life with a dose of Southern hospitality. These devotions started in a family text to intentionally set our morning focus on Jesus. They evolved into a larger audience of our church and community–and they are now being shared with you.

As an added bonus, you can connect with us through video links to learn more about our family foundations that led me to intentional faith. (And get a taste of some family recipes that are sure to tickle your fancy!)

# Dedication

This book is dedicated to the family who inspired its birth. Rodney, you are my best friend, my partner, and my cheerleader. Blake, Tyler and Jarrett, you are my greatest blessings. I love seeing the families you are building and watching God weave us all together in His perfect stiches. To all my extended family, especially those who came before me, thank you for the roots of faith that have been so firmly planted in our lives. Our love is imperfect, but it is woven by His perfect love. ♡

# Table of Contents for Video Links

*While this is a book of devotions, there are links to video chats embedded throughout the book. Scan the links to join Pam and many members of her family.*

"Change is good. You go first." This is one of my favorite quotes from the Dilbert comic strip. Isn't it accurate for our human selves? We can say, "Oooh, if that were me, I would…." We are good at saying what we would do when it isn't our situation. When it is our own turn to step out in faith, we suddenly get cold feet. Look at this scripture in Romans.

> "For in this hope we were saved. Now hope that is seen is
> not hope. For who hopes for what he sees? But if we hope
> for what we do not see, we wait for it with patience."
>
> Romans 8: 24-25 ESV

Let that one marinate in our minds for a minute. If we already know the ending before we ever take a step, real faith isn't required. Faith is believing in what we may not be able to see or prove on our own. Faith is being obedient to God's nudges in spite of the fact that there may be great risk or uncertainty. Faith is letting go and letting God–trusting God's will to prevail.

Easier said than done, right? Let's seek ways that God may be nudging us to step out in faith. Maybe it is an act of forgiveness or a major life change or a financial twist or a million other possible things. God says to seek Him and trust Him. He already knows the end of the story.

## Change is Good…You Go First

1

Have you ever seen a crack in floor tile? I have several hairline cracks in my bathroom. They drive me crazy. Sometimes those cracks are due to poor tile, but they are more often caused by some tiny shifts in the foundation. I am told it is called "settling."

What about our spiritual foundation? How strong is it? Do we know what we believe? Do we know God's word? His promises? His directives?

What happens when daily life comes in and causes cracks in our foundation? What happens when we face medical problems, loss of finances, or family distress? What happens when our faith is tested? Do we let Satan sneak in to try to widen those cracks, or do we seek God's face and let His love pour into those spaces?

> "Therefore, thus says the Lord God, "Behold, I am the one who has laid as a foundation in Zion, a stone, a tested stone, a precious cornerstone, of a sure foundation: 'Whoever believes will not be in haste.'"
>
> Isaiah 28:16 ESV

God is as close as the mention of His name, and He is our solid rock. ♡

"Enjoy the good, outlast the bad, and don't sweat the in-between."

I read this quote, and I thought of life. It is often a series of hills and valleys and the climb or fall from one to another. Guess what? God is with us through it all. He does not walk away. We must look for Him. We must listen to Him. We must focus on Him.

> "Even though I walk through the valley of the shadow of death, I will fear no evil, for you are with me; your rod and your staff, they comfort me."
>
> Psalm 23:4 ESV

Satan would love nothing better than to send us a storm, weakening our faith or driving a wedge in our relationship with God. That is why we must be vigilant to look, listen, and focus. Be encouraged today no matter where you are in life. God is with us. Seek Him, and cling to His promises. ♡

Do you sometimes find yourself in a revolving routine? Early morning alarm, juggling a million tasks during the day, returning home from work with a multitude of jobs waiting for you—only to begin it all again the next day?

Life can become super busy and sometimes stressful. God didn't intend for our gift of life to be this way. Look at these verses:

> "The Lord is my shepherd; I shall not want. He makes me lie down in green pastures. He leads me beside still waters. He restores my soul. He leads me in paths of righteousness for his name's sake."
>
> Psalm 23:1-3 ESV

Breathe that in. God intends for us to stop and refocus, slow down and reset. Wouldn't it be nice to literally sit in the grass or gaze at water? Then why don't we? We say we don't have time, but is that true?

Why don't we have time? Could it be our priorities? Could it be that we have said yes to too many things? Could it be that we have been blessed with so much that we have consistently added too much to our plates—by our own choices?

With everything going on in this world today, it is clearer than ever that life is a gift... a blessing to be cherished. Let's make time this week to really examine how we are spending each day. Are we allowing ourselves time to let God restore our souls? ♡

"Hey! Wait for me!" Have you ever had to wait on someone or something? How did that go for you? Is waiting a normal routine for you? Does it try your patience or are you able to roll with it?

Sooooo, have you ever had to wait on God? Have you prayed and prayed for answers and met silence? Consider this:

*Waiting is not passive. Waiting is meant to be a time of preparation, a time for rest and healing.*

Hmmm. I have found that waiting is one of the toughest measures of faith. Waiting is NOT passive. I am a person of action, a fixer, a check-the-box person. God has had me in a season of waiting. I am learning and trusting and growing. I am resting and healing in Him. I am waiting. It isn't easy, but I am taking notes.

> "Be patient, therefore, brothers, until the coming of the Lord. See how the farmer waits for the precious fruit of the earth, being patient about it, until it receives the early and the late rains. You also, be patient. Establish your hearts, for the coming of the Lord is at hand. Do not grumble against one another, brothers, so that you may not be judged; behold, the Judge is standing at the door. As an example of suffering and patience, brothers, take the prophets who spoke in the name of the Lord. Behold, we consider those blessed who remained steadfast. You have heard of the steadfastness of Job, and you have seen the purpose of the Lord, how the Lord is compassionate and merciful."
> James 5:7-11 ESV

This scripture speaks of waiting for His timing and His purpose. Take comfort that waiting is an act of faith when it involves waiting on God's direction. Be patient.♡

Have you ever watched a good wrestling match? My son wrestled in middle school, and I never could figure out how the wrestlers earned points. I was always engrossed in watching the event.

I recently went to the state wrestling tournament to support students, and those were some intense matches! It is always interesting to watch the athletes move from being the aggressor to being more passive while trying to figure out the next move.

I can't help but wonder if that is how we are with God sometimes. Do we wrestle with God over the work He is trying to do in our lives? Do we wrestle with the direction He is pointing out for us? Are we actively wrestling today, or are we pausing to catch our breath and looking for a way out?

> "For this light momentary affliction is preparing for us an eternal weight of glory beyond all comparison, as we look not to the things that are seen but to the things that are unseen. For the things that are seen are transient, but the things that are unseen are eternal."
>
> 2 Corinthians 4:17-18 ESV

We will never fully understand some pieces of our journey on this side of Heaven. Some of our life struggles will simply not make sense until we are past them and can look back and see God's hand at work. These are the times when our faith must be strong enough to step out and trust God even more than ever. ♡

Does the acronym WWJD mean anything to you? If you were a kid (or the parent of a kid) in the early 2000s, you will remember this as a popular term. It was on t-shirts and wristbands. "What would Jesus do?" It is a good question to measure our actions: What WOULD Jesus do?

I find myself still using this "measure" today. When I find myself in a tough situation, I often ask what Jesus would do if He were in my shoes. (I guess, technically, He is.) As a Christian, He is always in my heart, even when I may not be thinking of Him. Sometimes I just get tired–tired of all the ugly and the sin (my own included), and it seems that the world is falling apart. Sometimes it feels that my little efforts to live for Jesus are just not enough.

> "Do not be deceived: God is not mocked, for whatever one sows, that will he also reap. For the one who sows to his own flesh will from the flesh reap corruption, but the one who sows to the Spirit will from the Spirit reap eternal life. And let us not grow weary of doing good, for in due season we will reap, if we do not give up. So then, as we have opportunity, let us do good to everyone, and especially to those who are of the household of faith."
> Galatians 6:7-10 ESV

If you get discouraged in your Christian faith when you look at the news or media or talk with peers, take heart! Do NOT get tired of being the Good! Do NOT give up! Live for Jesus every day! Live out our faith! Be the light! Let others see Jesus in you and through you! ♡

Have you ever seen or heard something that you could not understand? Maybe you have witnessed a baby being born and were awed by the miracle of it. Maybe you have seen a piece of architecture that seems impossible, yet it stands. Maybe you have heard a song that moves you to tears, yet you don't understand a word of it because it is in a different language.

We will see and hear things in life that we don't understand. The same will be true in our spiritual walks. Look at this verse:

> "But as it is written, what no eye has seen, nor ear heard, nor the heart of man imagined, what God has prepared for those who love him."
>
> 1 Corinthians 2:9 ESV

God has a plan for our lives, but the plan may not always make sense. We don't see the big picture; God does. Our minds cannot fully comprehend like God can, and there are going to be times that we feel Him leading us through paths that we do not understand. These are the times that we must walk in faith. We must trust. ♡

Are you a mind reader? I recall as a child that my Daddy would get quite frustrated with my lack of mechanical mind when I could not anticipate which tool he would need next. I was sooooo not a mind reader.

On the other hand, my children often found it uncanny how I could anticipate some of their thoughts. The good old parental "gut instinct" came in quite handy more than once.

Here is a thought to consider: We don't know God's plans. We are one very small piece of His infinite plan. We see a thread of the big picture while he is the designer of the entire tapestry.

> "For my thoughts are not your thoughts, neither are your ways my ways, declares the Lord. For as the heavens are higher than the earth, so are my ways higher than your ways and my thoughts than your thoughts."
> Isaiah 55:8-9 ESV

I don't pretend to understand God's plan every day. I will even admit that sometimes I don't like parts of the plan, but I work really hard to push against my own selfish ways in order to trust that His plan is best.

One day at a time.

Sometimes one breath at a time. ♡

Do you ever get tired of inviting folks to church? Do you grow weary with the family for whom you pray daily and still resist a close relationship with God? Do you get frustrated with friends who continually fall back into unhealthy ruts after multiple conversations of support?

These struggles are real, but they are not new. Imagine the life of Paul and Timothy and Peter and John–and so many others from the *Bible*.

> "And the Lord said, "You pity the plant, for which you did not labor, nor did you make it grow, which came into being in a night and perished in a night. And should not I pity Nineveh, that great city, in which there are more than 120,000 persons who do not know their right hand from their left, and also much cattle?""
>
> Jonah 4:10-11 ESV

Jonah was sent on a mission to share God's love and message with these people. Jonah resisted. He didn't feel the same way about the people in Nineveh. After the message was finally delivered to them, he sat down outside of the city under the shade of a tree to cool down. The plant was miraculously placed there by God for Jonah. In the same token, God sent a worm to eat through the plant the very next day so that Jonah could learn an important lesson. He mourned the loss of this plant even though he had done nothing to help it grow. He had invested nothing in it, yet Jonah wanted God to just give up on these folks in Nineveh because they were being stubborn. God loved these people (much like He loves us) and He wasn't giving up on them.

Ouch. I am so very thankful that God did not give up on me. I still mess up on a regular basis and He still loves me and guides me. We must learn to be patient with our neighbors and family and friends who may be slow to embrace Jesus. They are God's creations as well, and He has plans for their lives, too. We may even be the "Jonah" who is sent to share a message (maybe more than once). We must remember that none of us are perfect, and we must be obedient to the nudges God sends us as workers for Him. His plans and His time...♡

•  •  •

## Do you ever tire of inviting people to Jesus?

Have you ever told a little white lie? What about a whopping big lie or even one of those tricky lies of omission?

If we are all honest with ourselves, that answer is likely *yes*. We are weak humans who sometimes avoid the truth for a large variety of reasons. This makes life quite painful for all of us whether we are telling or receiving a lie.

Did you know that God does not lie? Did you know that God cannot lie? Look at this scripture:

> "So when God desired to show more convincingly to the heirs of the promise the unchangeable character of his purpose, he guaranteed it with an oath, so that by two unchangeable things, in which it is impossible for God to lie, we who have fled for refuge might have strong encouragement to hold fast to the hope set before us."
>
> Hebrews 6:17-18 ESV

Did you see it? Because it is impossible for God to lie, we can hold fast to the hope He gives us. God's promises are true! He loves us. He is here.

> "Have I not commanded you? Be strong and courageous. Do not be frightened, and do not be dismayed, for the Lord your God is with you wherever you go."
>
> Joshua 1:9 ESV

Take heart today! If God said it, then it is TRUE! Rest in His truth today! ♡

*Faithful.* What does that mean to you–loyal? worthy of trust? secure?

One of my favorite hymns is "Great is Thy Faithfulness." God is faithful. He is consistent. He can be counted on. He is here–always.

> "Let us hold fast the confession of our hope without wavering, for He who promised is faithful."
>
> Hebrews 10:23 ESV

> "God is faithful, by whom you were called into the fellowship of his Son, Jesus Christ our Lord."
>
> 1 Corinthians 1:9 ESV

Isn't it amazing to know that no matter where we are in our journey, God is there? No matter what life may toss our way, God is there. Take heart today, and rest in His faithfulness. His promises are true, and His presence is faithful. ♡

Can you do a backflip? Are you one of those who loves roller coasters that go backwards?

While neither of those examples are descriptive of me, there is a "back" word that does fit me (and likely you). Have you heard of *backsliding*? It is defined as the action of relapsing into bad ways. I am guilty–are you?

We get focused on Christ and work to share His love with others, and then life happens. Maybe temptation comes our way or hectic schedules make us lose our focus. Regardless, we backslide. God knew this would be a problem. Look at this verse:

> "Watch and pray that you may not enter into temptation.
> The spirit indeed is willing, but the flesh is weak."
> Matthew 26:41 ESV

Aren't we glad that God stands strong beside us? Isn't it great He knows our hearts and our imperfections? Aren't we glad He forgives?

> "If people who are called by my name humble themselves
> and pray and seek my face and turn from their wicked ways,
> then I will hear from heaven and will forgive their sin and
> heal their land."
> 2 Chronicles 7:14 ESV

We are all imperfect human beings who are full of sin. It is only through God's grace that we receive eternal life. We will never earn it. It is His gift, and we are so blessed by it! ♡

Don't you love a good parade? Parades just have a sense of excitement and community spirit! Did you know there was a parade, a "glory" parade in the book of Exodus?

> "Moses said, 'Please show me your glory.' And he said, 'I will make all my goodness pass before you and will proclaim before you my name 'The Lord.' And I will be gracious to whom I will be gracious and will show mercy on whom I will show mercy'."
>
> Exodus 33:18-19 ESV

Moses wanted to see God's glory; Moses wanted to be in His presence. Moses was being asked to take some major steps of faith, and he was seeking close comfort with God.

There are some fundamentals that God expects us to follow as we seek Him, as we follow Him. Sometimes we don't particularly enjoy these parts of scripture because they step on our toes, but the fundamentals are there for us.

> "Or do you not know that the unrighteous will not inherit the kingdom of God? Do not be deceived: neither the sexually immoral, nor idolaters, nor adulterers, nor men who practice homosexuality, nor thieves, nor the greedy, nor drunkards, nor revilers, nor swindlers will inherit the kingdom of God. **And such were some of you**. But you were washed, you were sanctified, you were justified in the name of the Lord Jesus Christ and by the Spirit of our God."
>
> 1 Corinthians 6:9-11 ESV

Do you see that encouragement in verse 11? And some were such as you, BUT you were washed in Jesus's name. There is hope for us all. We are all sinners; we all fail; we all sin. Some sins are more public than others, but sin is sin. God knows and He guides and forgives–if we seek Him. ♡

# Fried Biscuits

5-6 leftover biscuits
2 large eggs
½ cup sugar
Oil for frying
Jelly or Jam of your choice

Pour the oil into a frying pan and turn to medium-high heat. Oil should be ½ inch deep in your pan. Slice the biscuits open into two thin circular halves. Whisk the eggs and sugar in a bowl for dipping the biscuits. When the oil is sizzling, dredge a biscuit half through the egg mixture and drop it into the oil. (Do NOT leave the biscuit sitting in the egg mixture.) Repeat with subsequent biscuit slices. Flip the slices in the oil to allow for browning on both sides. Remove from oil and place on a paper towel to drain.

Serve with the jam or jelly of your preference. Our family loves to use fresh strawberry preserves.

Tips: Homemade (or frozen) biscuits work best, but canned can be used. In addition, you will likely need to reduce the heat to medium once you begin frying a second batch; otherwise, the oil tends to get too hot and burn the egg mixture.

Join me here and meet the hubby behind the camera. Rodney and I will prepare this dish together. :)

# Fried Biscuits

I come from a farm family of many generations. We have been taught to be frugal and avoid waste. These biscuits are a not-so-healthy treat that has been passed down through our family from the days when all biscuits were homemade and often became hard the next day. Frying them in an egg and sugar wash turned them into a softer and sweeter treat.

Join me here to make this tasty treat and to see the old pie safe built by my great-grandfather that was used to house day-old biscuits. (And finally meet Rodney, my hubby, who is my right hand!)

Have you ever heard of the 7 Degrees of Separation Phenomenon? It is the idea that everyone is connected much more closely than we realize. It explains how my hubby and son can travel from South Georgia to North Indiana and the customer behind them hears them speaking and asks if they are from Georgia…and then realizes she is a friend of mine from high school. It explains how no matter where we go it will not take us long to bump into someone we know or someone that links us to someone we know. The world isn't quite as large as we might sometimes think.

So, let's talk about our own "sphere of influence." Sometimes I get overwhelmed when I see the problems of our world, and I feel that I can't make a difference. I just feel that the problems are TOO big. Then I consider how interconnected we are. Maybe I–maybe WE–can make a difference.

Our pastor recently spoke of us standing on the sidewalk and drawing a chalk circle around ourselves. As he spoke of revival, he said it must begin inside that circle, inside our own hearts. First.

Imagine if we all drew that circle and prayed for revival within our own hearts, if we prayed for God to renew the fire for serving Him within our spirits. If we individually get excited, those circles will connect, and God can use us in mighty ways to positively impact this ole world.

I am standing in my circle, and I am praying. Would you like a piece of chalk, too? ♡

*Bitterness.* Not a pretty word, right? The word itself even leaves an unpleasant taste. What is the saying: "Bitterness can be a hard pill to swallow"?

All of us have likely experienced disappointments. There are moments when we have even been devastated by a turn of events. The question becomes, "Do these times become defining moments in our lives?"

Consider Naomi in the book of Ruth. She lost her husband and then both of her sons in the opening verses of chapter 1. In addition, she is left in a foreign land and must make her way back to her homeland. As Naomi and her daughter-in-law, Ruth, are entering her hometown, friends run to greet her. Look with me at Naomi's response.

> "She said to them, 'Do not call me Naomi; call me Mara, for the Almighty has dealt very bitterly with me. I went away full, and the Lord has brought me back empty. Why call me Naomi, when the Lord has testified against me and the Almighty has brought calamity upon me?'"
>
> Ruth 1:20-21 ESV

Whew. She is bitter. You can almost taste the bitterness in her words. She even wants them to call her Mara, which means *bitter*, because God has allowed these terrible things to happen.

I kinda get it. Don't you? I cannot imagine what she must have felt at this time. The pain and anguish of just placing one foot in front of the other must have seemed impossible.

Here is where I want us to pause and think. God redeemed Naomi and Ruth. He was faithful and provided for them in powerful ways. We may never know why Naomi's loss was so great, but we can read chapters 1-4 to see God's faithfulness through the valley. If you are experiencing a valley today, and the foul taste of bitterness is trying to delve into your soul, be encouraged and know that God is right here. ♡

Have you ever seen the 1998 movie *Saving Private Ryan*? It is a WWII movie that has received many awards for its realistic and heart-wrenching portrayal of D-Day. In a particular scene, Sarge tells Private Ryan to "earn this." Private Ryan was going to live and go on to build a life after this day while so many others were not. What a blessing!

What about us? Are we "earning" the blessing of life we have been given each day? Don't misunderstand: we cannot earn salvation as it is a gift from God. However, each day we get is also a gift of purpose, so are we seeking to serve God with each day, or are we taking them for granted?

Look at this verse:

> "Therefore, I urge you to walk in a manner worthy of your calling, for you have been called by God."
>
> Ephesians 4:1 ESV

Wow. I am called by God. You are called by God. What are we doing with our calls? Are we fulfilling our purposes? I challenge us all to seek to serve God by ministering to others in some small way today. ♡

Do you appreciate good service in a restaurant? How does it make you feel to sit down to have a meal and have someone who promptly and efficiently serves you? I think we have a greater appreciation for quality service when we have experienced poor service a few times.

Good service makes us feel valued and respected. Our overall experience becomes much more pleasurable.

Consider these verses from Joshua:

> "And if it is evil in your eyes to serve the Lord, choose this day whom you will serve, whether the gods your fathers served in the region beyond the river, or the gods of the Amorites in whose land you dwell. But as for me and my house, we will serve the Lord.""
>
> Joshua 24:15 ESV

I have often heard this verse, especially the last statement: "As for me and my house, we will serve the Lord." Maybe we even have it displayed somewhere in your house. Do we *mean* it?

Are we providing good service to God? Are we truly serving Him? Or are we making Him wait? Are we running around putting others first and giving Him what is left? Is God a priority or a second thought?

Are we making other gods (priorities) and putting them before the One True God? ♡

Are you a sharer? If you see a good sale of a product that your friend enjoys, do you call to share? During a shortage of baby formula, if you saw a large stock in a store, would you reach out to those who had babies to let them know it was available? Are you a sharer who is eager to brighten someone's day?

A recent Sunday School lesson gave me pause. A Christian felt burdened to share the plan of salvation with a long-time friend, but he was nervous and felt inept, so he gave his friend a pamphlet about Jesus and salvation. His friend read through it and looked up and said, "If this is true, I can't believe we have been friends all these years and you have never told me."

Are we sharing Jesus with others? Look at what Andrew did as soon as he met Jesus...

> "One of the two who heard John speak and followed Jesus was Andrew, Simon Peter's brother. He first found his own brother Simon and said to him, "We have found the Messiah" (which means Christ). He brought him to Jesus..."
> John 1:40-42 ESV

Andrew immediately went to tell his brother and then took him to meet Jesus. Andrew SHARED. Are we sharing Jesus today? ♡

Have you ever seen the sunrise? Isn't it a glorious sight? I love seeing the colors of the sky as it changes. The multitude of oranges and yellows emerge with whispers of pinks and begin changing the night sky to a swath of purples and blues.

To me, it is a sign of hope. The sunrise is a dependable, clean slate for a new day; it is like an awakening of a new opportunity in life.

Did you know that we have even greater hope in the Son-rise? Jesus died on the cross for our sins. Our mistakes are covered in His blood, and we have a new beginning in Him. He is our hope, our salvation.

Look in Matthew 24:

> "For as the lightning comes from the east and shines as far as the west, so will be the coming of the Son of Man."
>
> Matthew 24:27 ESV

Jesus died for us. Promise fulfilled. Jesus is coming for us. Promise of hope. ♡

"God sometimes pries our fingers from the things we clutch the hardest so that we have open hands to receive the things He longs to give us."

Wow. I read this statement recently, and I paused. Isn't this so very true? How often does this happen in our lives? How often do we miss it because of our own stubborn will?

> "For I know the plans I have for you, declares the Lord, plans for welfare and not for evil, to give you a future and a hope."
>
> Jeremiah 29:11 ESV

Coach John Wooden thought he needed to coach in his home state of Indiana, but God sent him to the UCLA Bruins where he made basketball history again and again.

In a World Series interview, Atlanta Brave Dansby Swanson spoke of his unwanted trade to Atlanta and the fact that God's plans were so much better than his own.

As I reflect on my own life, I can see where God has done the same for me at different times. If you are at a turning point in your life and are struggling with making change, seek God. Reflect to see if this moment could be from Him. If God is at work, trust Him. His plans are always better than our own. Release that grip and hold those hands open for God's way. ♡

Have you ever participated in a 50/50 raffle? These are easy fundraisers if people have generous hearts. The organization simply collects donations and draws a name, and the winner gets half of the money and the organization keeps the other half. Easy peasy, right?

Have you ever met someone with 50/50 commitment? You know those people who are going to take the side of the person who is standing there at the moment and then change sides when the person changes. Those kinds of folks cause me indigestion.

Are WE those kinds of folks? (Put on some sturdy shoes here because our toes are about to be stomped.) Are you "all in" for Jesus or are you a 50/50 person? Is your faith strong at church and weak at work? Does your faith run deep in prayer groups and run awry at family gatherings?

God is clear that we are to choose: Him or the world. There is no 50/50. Look at these words in Revelation:

> "'I know your works: you are neither cold nor hot. Would that you were either cold or hot! So, because you are lukewarm, and neither hot nor cold, I will spit you out of my mouth."
>
> Revelation 3:15-16 ESV

It is easy to have faith in calm waters. It is more difficult to stand firm when waves are crashing around us. I have room to improve. What about you? ♡

*All.* That is a big word. It may have only three letters, but it encompasses every single one— not some, not most— all.

Look at this verse:

> "For all have sinned and come short of the glory of God."
>
> Romans 3:23

Who has sinned? All. You...me... all. We are all sinners. Some of us may feel that our sins are bigger... worse... less forgivable... God says ALL have sinned and fall short of His glory.

> "None is righteous. No, not one."
>
> Romans 3:10.

None of us.... not even one of us... is perfect. Or even close. We are sinners. We let God down daily, yet He loves us and forgives us. ALL of us.

> "If we confess our sins, he is faithful and just to forgive us our sins, and to cleanse us from all unrighteousness."
>
> 1 John 1:9.

If we ever struggle with feeling that we have let God down, or we get in a comparison game of thinking that we are not as worthy of His love as others, stop. God created us, He loves us, He forgives us, and He wants a personal relationship with us. God loves us ALL! ♡

Do you ever get nervous about taking a test? Do you simply walk in and breeze through or do you experience anxiety about your success?

In every testing "season" for many students across our nation, I bet there are mixed feelings among these students (and teachers) as the tests begin. Some relish the opportunity to show what they have learned or taught while others cringe in worry.

I couldn't help but think today of the ultimate test: it is a single question test. It will come at death when we face our Father in Heaven. Will our names be in the Lamb's Book of Life? Will we hear, "Well done, my good and faithful servant?" Will we enter Heaven to spend eternity at the feet of Jesus?

> "Then I saw a great white throne and him who was seated on it. From his presence the earth and sky fled away, and no place was found for them. And I saw the dead, great and small, standing before the throne, and books were opened. Then another book was opened, which is the book of life. And the dead were judged by what was written in the books, according to what they had done."
>
> Revelation 20:11-12 ESV

There will be a day of judgment for each of us. The test question is simple, yet profound: Did I choose Jesus Christ as my Savior and choose to live for Him?

We will never be perfect, we will always be full of sin, but we can be changed forever when we choose to pursue life through the lens of Christ. ♡

Have you ever shared your love for Jesus with others and felt like it was ignored? Have you ever wondered if your Christian faith positively impacts others?

God taught me a new lesson this week. He used the story of Daniel and the lions' den. Most of us are familiar with the story: Daniel loved God. The king liked Daniel. The king signed a law that said no citizen can worship anyone BUT the king. Daniel continued praying to God daily (and did not try to hide it). Daniel was thrown into the lions' den. and God sealed the mouths of the lions and saved Daniel. Great story, right?

Here is what gave me pause. Look in chapter 6:

> "Then the king went to his palace and spent the night fasting; no diversions were brought to him, and sleep fled from him. Then, at break of day, the king arose and went in haste to the den of lions. As he came near to the den where Daniel was, he cried out in a tone of anguish. The king declared to Daniel, 'O Daniel, servant of the living God, has your God, whom you serve continually, been able to deliver you from the lions?'"
>
> Daniel 6:18-20 ESV

I always knew the king was upset that he had been tricked into signing a law that would harm Daniel. However, I had never really looked at the king's actions. He fasted… he wrestled… he remained alone all night… could it be that he sought the God that Daniel served? Could it be that he whispered something like, "God if you really do exist, please spare Daniel!" Could this night have been God at work in the king?

At daybreak the king goes running to the den and shouts to Daniel. Could it be that my focus all of these years has been on Daniel's unwavering faith and that I have missed the fact that the king is having a God moment of his own? Have all those seeds of faith that Daniel has planted again and again been heard?

Go read Daniel 6. Look for God at work... not only in Daniel, but also in the king. Be encouraged that your life is planting seeds in others today. You may never realize how God may use you to build relationships with others that will have a heavenly impact. ♡

•  •  •

## Daniel and the Lions Den: A Focus on the King

How do you like French fries: Steak cut, crinkle cut or shoestring? Battered or plain? I am a crinkle cut girl with a healthy sprinkling of salt! Yummy! A box of hot, salty fries from one of our local restaurants has often led to the demise of my dieting plans.

Did you know that God likes salt, too? Consider this scripture:

> "You are the salt of the earth, but if salt has lost its taste, how shall its saltiness be restored? It is no longer good for anything except to be thrown out and trampled under people's feet."
>
> Matthew 5:13 ESV

God is very clear. We are to be full of the flavor of Him. We are to have faith that has a taste that is clear. If we call ourselves Christians, but we simply mix in with the rest of the world, then we have no flavor, we are not set apart. I worry that in the culture of today that many folks are becoming bland with little flavor; Christians are not standing out nor apart. We don't bring seasonings to the table; we should have a flavor that draws others to God. Read that scripture again. Ponder on it... reflect on your own life. Are you salty for Christ? ♡

Are you a talker? Do you enjoy engaging in conversation with people? Did you know that some research finds the average person speaks over 10,000 words per day?

Whew! That is a lot of chit chat! What if, at the end of the day, we had a way to pause to look through everything we say in a day? Better yet, what if we could sit down with God to review these words together? What would He say? Would He be proud of what came from our mouths during the day?

I was humbled by this scripture recently. I read it and felt like God grabbed me by my collar and told me to read it again.

> "I tell you, on the day of judgment people will give account
> for every careless word they speak, for by your words you
> will be justified, and by your words you will be condemned."
> Matthew 12:36-37 ESV

It is scary to consider the power of our words. They can be used to build up or to tear down. We are to use them carefully. We are to speak the truth. We are to listen more than we speak. Today is a new day, a fresh start. Let's make our words count! ♡

Have you ever skipped rocks on water? It looks so cool! I cannot say that I have mastered the craft, but I surely do enjoy seeing others compete to see how many skips the stone can take before it sinks.

I also like to see the painted rocks that crafty folks place around town for others to find. These stones are sure to bring an extra sparkle to the day.

Jesus referenced stones, too. As Jesus was entering Jerusalem on Palm Sunday in the days before His crucifixion, the disciples and other believers were excitedly welcoming Him. They were making some noise; they were worshiping Him! Some folks didn't like it; they even told Jesus to make them hush and look at His response.

> "He answered, 'I tell you, if these were silent, the very stones would cry out'."
>
> Luke 19:40 ESV

Let's pause here. Who is louder in our lives: our worship or the stones? Are we making some noise? Are we worshiping in plain sight? Do others see Jesus in us?

I don't want rocks to have to cry out in my silence. ♡

Did you ever have an art teacher who gave you a lump of clay and let you mold it into a shape? I bet many of us fashioned adorable pots or pets to be used for trinkets or paperweights. Some of us may even have similar treasures that our children have brought home to us.

Go back to that lump of soft, pliable clay. Think of it as your own life and God is the one molding and shaping it. God wants to be such an integral part of our lives that we allow Him to direct us, shape us, grow us.

> "O house of Israel, cannot I do with you as this potter? saith
> the LORD. Behold, as the clay is in the potter's hand, so are
> ye in mine hand, O house of Israel."
>
> Jeremiah 18:6 KJV

It is only through daily contact with him in prayer, in Bible reading, in worship, that we can remain pliable, moldable. Without this daily relationship, our lump of clay begins to harden and set. We stop growing in faith and in love. ♡

What are your plans today? Do you have them mapped out in your head? Do your plans ever get derailed? Do you ever get frustrated when they do?

What about our life plans? These are bigger than a daily plan; these are often the plans that include our hopes and dreams. What happens when those seem to fall apart?

One of my favorite verses of comfort is:

> "For I know the plans I have for you, declares the Lord, plans for welfare and not for evil, to give you a future and a hope."
>
> Jeremiah 29:11 ESV

It is an amazing comfort to know that God has a plan for us. He knows what is best for us.

> "Trust in the Lord with all your heart, and do not lean on your own understanding. In all your ways acknowledge him, and he will make straight your paths."
>
> Proverbs 3:5-6 ESV

If you are struggling with events of life, trust God. Seek His face. Ask for His will. (His plan may not match our plan.) Seek discernment to know what steps to take. He will guide us, and His plans are always best. ♡

Have you ever had one of those nightmares in which you were trying to escape someone and no matter which way you turned, the person was there? (Hopefully, I am not the only one who has wild dreams sometimes.)

Consider another thought. Do you have a family member or friend who is always there for you? Someone who shows up in the good times and the bad to lend you comfort and support. We are blessed if we have folks like this.

Did you know that ALL of us can always have the most amazing person with us? Look at this scripture:

> "Where shall I go from your Spirit? Or where shall I flee from your presence? If I ascend to heaven, you are there! If I make my bed in Sheol, you are there! If I take the wings of the morning and dwell in the uttermost parts of the sea, even there your hand shall lead me, and your right hand shall hold me."
>
> Psalm 139:7-10 ESV

God is with us, everywhere, in the good and in the bad. Do I fully understand why some things happen? No, I don't. Do I sometimes have questions? Yes, I do. However, the Bible tells me again and again that God knows all, and He is never surprised because He is with me for every step. I simply need to focus on Him. ♡

I like to dabble in vegetables by planting a few (truly a few) things in spots of my flower beds so I can walk outside and pick a few squashes or cut some fresh okra and enjoy.

I walked out back for the first time in a few days and was startled. Some of my okra stalks were leafless and my sweet potato vines were sad. After faithfully tending these plants for several weeks, I fell away and could see the visible results.

I instantly thought of the old adage: "You reap what you sow." Did you know that came from the Bible?

> "Do not be deceived: God is not mocked, for whatever one sows, that will he also reap. For the one who sows to his own flesh will from the flesh reap corruption, but the one who sows to the Spirit will from the Spirit reap eternal life. And let us not grow weary of doing good, for in due season we will reap, if we do not give up."
>
> Galatians 6:7-9 ESV

As Christians, we will reap what we sow. We are to be planting seeds of faith in others while we also seek ways to nourish our own faith through Bible reading, prayer, and worship. Let's be intentional about sowing today. ♡

Who do you hang out with? Who do you choose to spend your free time with?

Have you ever paused to consider who Jesus hung out with? While Jesus encountered many people during his earthly years, he spent a lot of time with his disciples, the mixed bag of twelve personalities. Some who loved Him and believed Him immediately, others who loved Him and took a while to be convinced of His plan and even one who would be a traitor to Him.

Hmmm.... We could learn something here. This was Jesus: He knew their thoughts, their hearts, and He still poured into them. He modeled how to serve, how to love, how to correct. He taught, and he *re*taught.

The lesson that really stood out to me is that He gave these newborn Christians time to grow and make mistakes and learn. Do we? Do we see someone accept Christ and celebrate and then quickly judge the first time a stumble is made? Or do we support and love and reteach? Do we realize that we stumble, too? ♡

Have you ever been in a group with 60 million people? Hard to imagine, right? If you have been to a Braves game at Truist Park, you were with just over 41,000 people if it was full. If you have attended an SEC championship at the Mercedes Benz Stadium, you observed as one of 75,000 at capacity. Those are THOUSANDS... I am asking you to now imagine being seated with 60 MILLION.

Since Roe v. Wade was established in 1973, over 60 million babies have been aborted. Can you imagine what those lives might have accomplished? The problems that might have been solved by some of them? (The decision to have an abortion is not easy and many who make that choice struggle with it for years beyond. We all have decisions we wish we could undo; aren't we thankful that God loves and forgives?)

The US Supreme Court voted to overturn Roe v. Wade. This will cause heated discussions; the decision will now lie in every state. We are to be praying! We are to stand on God's word and follow His lead.

There are rumors of violence that may spawn from this decision. Christians, pray. Pray for God to give you words in your own discussions. Pray for God to give wisdom and protection to those in harm's way. Pray that our country collectively seeks God's face and walks in His direction. Pray for the days to come. ♡

How fast can you walk/run a mile? (I bet some of you just laughed out loud, right?)

I have heard teens and adults speak of trying to get a six-minute mile or less. I am just excited if I go out to walk with *no* time kept.

Have you heard of the Christian "smile mile"?

> "And if anyone forces you to go one mile, go with him two miles."
>
> Matthew 5:41 ESV

A large part of this chapter is Jesus sharing that Christians are to be servants. We are to go the extra mile, go beyond the expected, show up, be there, be the hands and feet of Him.

Whether with family or friends, work or church, strangers or enemies, we are to go the extra steps. Love our enemies and forgive those who wrong us.

Those are some tall orders, right? Yep. Sometimes they cause me to swallow hard, too. God isn't saying to forsake His teachings by letting people just run over us, but He is saying we can stand in His Word AND show grace and love while doing it. That is the extra mile. Are we walking it today? ♡

# Bread Pudding

1 loaf of bread (or the equivalent in buns, biscuits, etc.)
3 cups sugar
1 tbsp cinnamon
1 stick butter
6 eggs
1 tbsp vanilla flavoring
1 tsp almond flavoring
3 cups milk

Tear the bread into small chunks. Add the cinnamon and sugar. Pour in a stick of melted butter. Add 6 large eggs and stir. Add vanilla and almond flavorings and milk and stir again. Heat the oven to 375° and pour the mixture into a LARGE greased baking pan. Bake for 35-40 minutes until golden brown. Remove from oven and sprinkle cinnamon sugar over the top. Slice into bite-size pieces.

Tips: This is a great recipe to mix the night before and refrigerate until morning. Then stir well and proceed with baking in the morning for a hot treat! If you use leftover doughnuts or something equally sweet and oily, reduce the amount of sugar and omit the butter.

# Bread Pudding

This, too, is a recipe of frugalness that has been passed down in my family. We have embraced the idea of "want not, waste not" over the years. If we have any type of bread that is a tad old, we whip up a batch of this scrumptious treat and share it at work, church or home. Click on the code to join me!

Have you ever talked smack? You talk big, but when it comes to action, you aren't quite as eager.

Aren't we sometimes this way with our faith? It can be easy to have faith when life is going well. It is frightening how weak that faith can become in the face of fear. We aren't the only ones. Here is an example with Peter.

> "And Peter answered him, "Lord, if it is you, command me to come to you on the water." He said, "Come." So, Peter got out of the boat and walked on the water and came to Jesus. But when he saw the wind, he was afraid, and beginning to sink he cried out, "Lord, save me." Jesus immediately reached out his hand and took hold of him, saying to him, "O you of little faith, why did you doubt?""
>
> Matthew 14:28-31 ESV

Peter is often known for his bold, outspoken personality. It is not surprising that he steps out of the boat without hesitation. He is stepping out in faith with confidence in Jesus until Peter takes his focus elsewhere. As Peter is walking across that water, he begins to notice the winds, the waves, and probably his own feet. Panic sets in and belief— faith—becomes weak.

Notice that the only thing that changed is Peter. Jesus remained the same from the first step to the last. It is Peter who shifted in thought and in action. How often is this us? How often do we lose focus on Jesus? We can trust in Him. ♡

What do you do with your anger? Yes, you read that correctly. What do you do with your anger? We all experience it at times. The question is what do we do with it?

Some folks spew it like a water hose while others hold onto it until it blows like a volcano. Still others wear it in hiding and pretend all is well while silently taking it out to examine it from time to time as it gnaws at them. Do any of these descriptions sound familiar?

Look with me in Ephesians 4 to see what God says we are to do:

> "Therefore, having put away falsehood, let each one of you speak the truth with his neighbor, for we are members one of another. Be angry and do not sin; do not let the sun go down on your anger," Ephesians 4:25-26 ESV

I see two big lessons here:

We are to be truthful, even when it is uncomfortable, even when the truth may hurt to hear (or to say). We are not to avoid difficult conversations just because they are, well, difficult.

We aren't to hold onto anger. It does not mean we cannot be angry. (We are sinful, imperfect humans who are going to make others angry. It is going to happen.) The lesson is that we are called to deal with it and soon. We are not to allow it to fester and grow and eat at us from inside.

Hmmm. Great scripture. Easier to read than to do, maybe? Anger can ruin relationships, divide families, and raise walls of distance. More importantly, anger can steal joy, shift focus, and color the lens through which we see the world. God does not want this for us. ♡

Have you ever noticed the disruption of good intentions? You know, like when you have committed to a diet and then a friend brings you an amazing dessert, or when you have committed to exercise after work and suddenly you have commitments every afternoon? Maybe your good intentions are even more serious, like committing to step away from a group of friends or family who are leading you the wrong way or going "cold turkey" on a habit that is not good for you. Have you noticed that when we commit to doing the "right" thing that temptation or insecurity seems to slap us in the face?

Friends, that is not accidental. The devil does not like for us to do anything that draws us closer to God. He is quite content if we are freely making a mess in our lives, so he can focus on destroying others. However, as soon as we step closer to God, to allow Him to fold us into His loving arms and experience His peace and joy, the devil goes on alert. He will do whatever is needed to try to steer us away from God.

> "10 Finally, be strong in the Lord and in the strength of his might. 11 Put on the whole armor of God, that you may be able to stand against the schemes of the devil. 12 For we do not wrestle against flesh and blood, but against the rulers, against the authorities, against the cosmic powers over this present darkness, against the spiritual forces of evil in the heavenly places. 13 Therefore take up the whole armor of God, that you may be able to withstand in the evil day, and having done all, to stand firm."
>
> Ephesians 6: 10-13 ESV

It is no accident that there are numerous scriptures to warn us against the ways of the devil. God knows we are imperfect and weak. God also knows the devil will use whatever he can to keep us from God. God gave us His Word to remind us that we must be on guard.

If you are dealing with insecurities or temptations today, stop and seek God's face. Put on His armor and know that there is no battle too large for Him. We are weak, but He is strong. Lean into His everlasting arms and send the devil scurrying away.

●  ●  ●

## The Disruption of Good Intentions

Have you ever tasted a green persimmon? What about sour candy? I bet if you have then your mouth is reacting as you read this. These things turn your mouth inside-out and cause you to want to spit...it...out!

Did you know God has a similar scenario? In Revelation chapters 2&3 we see descriptions of several churches from God's perspective. The final one is called Laodicea and this is what God says about it:

"15 I know your deeds, that you are neither cold nor hot. I wish you were either one or the other! 16 So, because you are lukewarm—neither hot nor cold—I am about to spit you out of my mouth."

As Christians we have a responsibility to live for Jesus. We are to be the hands and feet of the message of God. The Great Commission in Matthew 28:19 tells us to go make disciples of all nations, baptizing them in the name of the Father, Son and Holy Ghost. While we may not be the person performing baptisms, we can surely be the lights that point people to Jesus. ♡

Is prayer your steering wheel or your spare tire?

I saw this statement on social media and couldn't help but pause. I like to think Jesus is my steering wheel every single moment of every day, but honesty forced me to admit that my focus can veer.

In 2005 Carrie Underwood released the award-winning song called, "Jesus Take the Wheel." The lyrics are powerful. I even hear folks sometimes humorously say, "Jesus, take the wheel!"

The thought that keeps spinning in my head today is, "Do we mean it?" It is so easy to say things, but it takes so much more effort to commit to doing.

> "Rejoice always, pray without ceasing,"
>
> 1 Thessalonians 5:16-17 ESV

We are to pray, every day, frequently. Seek God's will. Follow His lead. Let Him take the wheel. ♡

*Worship.* What does this word mean to you? What does worship look like to you? Is it listening to a soul-gripping sermon? Is it rejoicing in music? Is it a head bent in prayer? Is it allowing the Word to seep into your soul? What is worship?

Genesis 22:5 is the first time the word "worship" is used in the Bible. It is used again over 8000 times. Yep. 8000 and counting. God wants us to worship Him. He wants our focus to be on Him, every. single. day.

The scripture in Genesis 22 introduces worship through obedience. Abraham was going to worship God by being obedient to God's direction. I had never really thought about obedience being a type of worship. It is self-sacrificial; it is the act of putting God ahead of ourselves. It is what Jesus did for us on the cross. God's direction is always the right direction. ♡

Have you begun investing in retirement? Do you have vacation savings or a Christmas account? We are certainly encouraged to prepare for the future.

Sometimes that preparation can cross over into hoarding. Sometimes our generosity is limited by our expanding wants. "I want a new boat, so I'm not contributing to the mission project this year." "I want to take a grand vacation, so I am skipping my tithe this month." Statements like these are common if we are truthful. Look at what God says:

> "And he (the man) said, 'I will do this: I will tear down my barns and build larger ones, and there I will store all my grain and my goods. And I will say to my soul, "Soul, you have ample goods laid up for many years; relax, eat, drink, be merry."' But God said to him, 'Fool! This night your soul is required of you, and the things you have prepared, whose will they be?' So is the one who lays up treasure for himself and is not rich toward God.'"
>
> Luke 12:18-21 ESV

Gulp. That last phrase gave me pause, "not rich toward God." I have a retirement plan and a "rainy day" savings for those unexpected expenses like replacing a broken appliance or vehicle part. I don't think God is opposed to this if I am not being generous to myself and stingy toward Him. I must pause and consider the spirit in which I serve God financially. Am I freely giving to the projects and needs that He places before me, or am I avoiding those opportunities in order to store money for myself? This is likely a look in the mirror that we all need to take. God's Word is clear. Look around today for opportunities to serve His work. ♡

"For God so loved…" Can you finish that verse with me? It is quite familiar to many.

> ""For God so loved the world, that he gave his only Son, that whoever believes in him should not perish but have eternal life."
>
> John 3:16 ESV

Were you able to recite it? Maybe you even knew the scripture address? The real question for us all is do we believe it?

God sent Jesus to show us the way to Him; Jesus taught us the way and then died for our sins so that we can receive God's grace.

Maybe you are reading and thinking that God couldn't have meant you. Oh, yes, He did. God loves you. He created you. He also gave you a choice: will you choose to live for Him?

Look at the verse immediately after John 3:16.

> "For God did not send his Son into the world to condemn the world, but in order that the world might be saved through him."
>
> John 3:17 ESV

God didn't send Jesus to condemn the world, so why do we sometimes condemn ourselves? Why do we allow Satan to convince us that we aren't worthy of God's love?

God loves us. He knows we are imperfect, that we are sinners. We have the choice to lean on God and trust Him, or to trust the world. Choose Jesus today. Give Him your heart, invite Him to reside there, and let His love flow into all parts of your life. ♡

Have you ever tasted flat soda? There surely is a big difference between carbonated water and plain water! The discovery of Coca Cola as we know it today was quite accidental. Its original purpose was medicinal. (Yes, I am a bit of a history nerd.)

But seriously, isn't it interesting that the change of one ingredient can be the difference in us savoring a swallow or wanting to spew it out?

Look at these verses in Revelation 3:

> "I know your works: you are neither cold nor hot. Would that you were either cold or hot! So, because you are lukewarm, and neither hot nor cold, I will spit you out of my mouth."
>
> Revelation 3:15-16 ESV

This is a powerful picture from God. I don't want to be a person that causes God to want to "spew me out." We had an interesting lesson in Sunday School recently that gave us insight about the water systems of that time in history and why this was the perfect analogy to use to get the Laodiceans to understand God's frustration.

I worry. I worry that on some days I am lukewarm, that I have lost my fizz. It takes work and commitment to keep God at the focus of our daily walks. We are here for a purpose and that is to share His love, daily. Thankfully, each day is a new opportunity to share Jesus! ♡

What is the definition of *bold*? What does it mean to BE bold?

Look at this definition:

Bold: showing an ability to take risks; confident, courageous

How BOLD are our prayer lives? Are we praying for requests half-heartedly? Are we praying for only those things that we can somewhat control?

Our Sunday School lesson was from 1 Kings 17-18 about the story of Elijah. He prayed **boldly** for a drought to help people turn toward God. He was obedient when God told him to go to the home of the widow and her son. Elijah prayed **boldly** for God to spare the life of the widow's son. He prayed **boldly** for the rain to return. Elijah prayed for fire to burn the sacrifice and the wet wood.

We have so much we can learn from Elijah about dependence on God and deep faith that bubbles forth with bold prayers. Go read these chapters today. Be encouraged. Step out in faith. ♡

Do you ever struggle in deciding what to wear? Do you seek comfort or fashion? Is there ever a day when nothing seems to suit you?

The fact that we have options of what to wear is a blessing. It is likely that most of us have way more than we need. While God may not care if we choose silk or cotton (and aren't we glad sackcloth is not a requirement), He did give some specific directions to believers.

> "In its place you have clothed yourselves with a brand-new nature that is continually being renewed as you learn more and more about Christ who created this new nature within you."
>
> Colossians 3:10

God said we as Christians are to be clothed in a new nature that is constantly evolving to become more and more like Christ as we deepen our walk with Him.

> "...you must clothe yourselves with tender-hearted mercy, kindness, humility, gentleness and patience."
>
> Colossians 3:12

Whew! Those are some tough clothes to fit into. The world is not going to be easy or fair; we are going to be wronged at times, even when we do our best to do what is right. In the same way that God continually shows us mercy and redirects us back to Him, we are to show this mercy and patience to others as we redirect them toward God. ♡

Are you an oak tree or a willow tree? I was asked and wasn't sure where the speaker was going with it. I like to see willow trees as they bend and flow with the wind. I also like to see the strong, towering oaks as they stand proudly through storm after storm.

Consider these trees when we consider our faith. Are we like the willow and easily "bend" our Biblical values when they are challenged, or do we stand strong like an oak and hold true to God's teaching?

What would Jesus have us to do? Let's look at how he reacted:

> "When many of his disciples heard it, they said, 'This is a hard saying; who can listen to it?' But Jesus, knowing in himself that his disciples were grumbling about this, said to them, 'Do you take offense at this'?"
>
> John 6:60-61 ESV

Jesus was teaching His followers about living a God-focused life. Some were not happy with the conversation.

> "It is the Spirit who gives life; the flesh is no help at all. The words that I have spoken to you are spirit and life. But there are some of you who do not believe."
>
> John 6:63-64 ESV

Do you see this? Jesus is being the "oak." He is not bending even though some folks are not agreeing with Him.

> "After this many of his disciples turned back and no longer walked with him. So, Jesus said to the twelve, 'Do you want to go away as well'?"
>
> John 6:66-67 ESV

Whew. This is when the going gets tough. Not only did Jesus stand strong even when it meant that He May lose some "friends," but He then turned to his closest friends and asked where they stood.

We have lessons to learn from this. Being a Christian means loving and serving and growing, but it also means standing on God's Word while doing it. It means we may have to stand alone at times. We may not be included with friends sometimes, and we may even lose some friends. Jesus lost friends, too. He still stood on the truth. We can, too. ♡

● ● ●

## Are you an oak or a willow?

Have you ever tried to take a nap while a fly buzzes around? Isn't it SO aggravating? There are just some things in life that drive us mad! Maybe it is a traffic jam or wrong directions, maybe it is gnats during the summer or mosquitoes on those glorious summer nights. Regardless, there are some things that test our patience.

I recently read a story of Corrie ten Boom during the time that she and her sister were imprisoned in a concentration camp during the Holocaust. They were Christians who had been caught hiding Jews when the Nazis were hunting them down. (Her book is called *The Hiding Place*.)

These two ladies were forced into a horrifying situation because they had tried to do the right thing. They were living in filthy barracks that were overrun by FLEAS and LICE.

One day Corrie was whining about their situation and her sister, Betsy, shared a powerful point. Betsy reminded Corrie that because of the fleas and lice in that barracks, no Nazi soldier wanted to enter for fear of contamination. As a result, these two sisters were able to run a ministry for every person who was sent to live there.

Wow. God sent an aggravation so that salvation could be shared. Could He do that at times for us? Could a flat tire on the side of the road be an opportunity to share Jesus with a stranger? Could a forced change at work put us near new people who need to hear about Jesus?

Next time we have an "aggravation" in front of us, let's take time to back up and look at the big picture. Maybe God is at work, and we have the glorious opportunity to be part of His plan. ♡

Have you ever seen a toddler "hide" by covering both eyes? Those babies think that if they cannot see us, then surely we cannot see them.

Funny, right? We are much like those toddlers. We often think that we have secrets, that our actions or thoughts are hidden from others.

Jesus said it isn't so.

> "Nothing is covered up that will not be revealed or hidden that will not be known. Therefore, whatever you have said in the dark shall be heard in the light, and what you have whispered in private rooms shall be proclaimed on the housetops."
>
> Luke 12:2-3 ESV

It is uncomfortable to consider that God knows everything. It is amazing to know that He loves us anyway. God will redirect, correct, forgive and love. ♡

Did you ever build things with modeling clay? As a child, I loved to play with many colors to make all kinds of creations. As an adult, I sometimes cringe to see the kids playing with it because I never know where little pieces of it may land.

I do still love the creativity and inspiration that can come from taking a lump of this and molding it into works of art. Isn't God the same with us?

> "O house of Israel, can I not do with you as this potter has done? declares the Lord. Behold, like the clay in the potter's hand, so are you in my hand, O house of Israel."
>
> Jeremiah 18:6 ESV

God wants to mold us into the special creation He has created us to be. We have to be willing to follow His lead.

> "The Lord will fulfill his purpose for me; your steadfast love, O Lord, endures forever. Do not forsake the work of your hands."
>
> Psalm 138:8 ESV

We are each created for a purpose in God's plan. Will we soften our hearts and humble ourselves enough to let Him take the lead? ♡

How is your week going? Is it chaotic or calm? Is it relaxing or stressful?

Jesus had a wild week many years ago. On Sunday, He rode into Jerusalem on a donkey and by Friday He was on a cross. I wonder how His Wednesday was going.

Some struggles in life come completely unexpectedly and steal our very breath. There are other struggles that we can see on the horizon, and we are not sure how we will take the steps necessary to get through them.

Jesus set a good example during that week. He showed humility. He gathered with Christian friends for support. He encouraged those around Him. Most importantly, He sought the Father through prayer.

> "And going a little farther he fell on his face and prayed, saying, 'My Father, if it be possible, let this cup pass from me; nevertheless, not as I will, but as you will'."
>
> Matthew 26:39 ESV

Jesus came as a human, and He had struggles as well. He understands.

Sunday is coming. ♡

# Juju's Peanut Butter Icing

16 oz jar creamy peanut butter
8 oz can sweetened condensed milk
1 cup of powdered sugar

Prepare cake layers first. Use whatever recipe or box mix, like me) that suits you.

Add peanut butter and sweetened condensed milk to the saucepan and turn on LOW heat. Stir until thoroughly mixed. Slowly add powdered sugar. (It works best if you use a sifter to avoid clumps. However, the taste is not affected either way.) Immediately begin spreading over layers. Add milk a tablespoon at the time if it is too thick to spread until you get the right consistency.

● ● ●

## Juju's Peanut Butter Cake

Join my sister and me as we make Mama's signature sweet and reminisce about our summers in the tobacco fields.

Have you ever wanted a "do-over"? Have you ever made such a mess that the only way you can find out is if you could just start over? We all have some of these experiences. The prophet Daniel found his country to be in quite a mess and knew that times were about to get tough. Look at how he handled his burden:

> "Then I turned my face to the Lord God, seeking him by prayer and pleas for mercy with fasting and sackcloth and ashes."
>
> Daniel 9:3 ESV

Daniel sees the direction his land is headed in and he is burdened. Sound familiar? What can we learn from Daniel's response?

1. Turn to the Lord… first… always.
2. Sacrifice may be required. (He fasted and was uncomfortable in sackcloth and ashes. His full focus was on God.)
3. We are all guilty. No one is without sin… no, not one. (If you continue reading Daniel, you will see that he uses the pronoun "we." Even though Daniel loved God and was seeking His face, Daniel realized that he had sin as well. We all do.

I am burdened most days by the news, social media and even conversations. Some days I simply want to throw my hands up and move far, far away from the mess of our world. However, God said there would be days like this. He said we are to turn from our wicked ways and call His name. (2 Chronicles 7:14) He will hear us. If you are burdened today, join me in prayer. He is listening. ♡

Where do you usually pray? In your bed? At meals? In your church?

When do you tend to pray? In the morning? Before bed? At church?

Consider this quote:

"The posture of your body doesn't matter as much as the posture of your soul. "

I heard this in a sermon, and it spoke to me. Some people get confused by thinking that prayer must be done in a certain manner with certain words. God cares much more about the heart than the how.

Pray out loud while driving down the road with your eyes wide open. Pray silently while you walk through your workplace. Pause to whisper a prayer before entering a meeting. Pray at the altar at church. Pray internally for a troubled friend you see from a distance in a store. Go chat with that same friend and ask if you can pray with him or her right then. The opportunities for prayer are wide open.

The time and the place do not matter nearly as much as the heart from which the prayer comes. Are our prayer lives simply going through the motions, or are we truly engaging with God? Today is a great day to start anew. ♡

"Lord, let me go running."

Are there things in your life that you say you will do, one day? Maybe you plan to save money, *one day*. Maybe you plan to travel, *one day*. Maybe you just look forward to resting, *one day*.

I am at an age where retirement is in the shorter rather than longer range. For some, this is the time that the "one day" dreams can come true. For others it seems that it can become an attitude of "I've done my part. Let others do it now."

What is your mindset in living for Christ? Are you saying you will "do it one day" or are you saying, "I've done my part. It is somebody else's turn now"? Neither of those options is what God asks of us. God wants our commitment, our energy, our work, now. We are to share His love, his salvation plan for eternal life with others, every day.

There is an old hymn titled, "We'll Work 'til Jesus Comes," and we can learn much from it. When it is our time to go meet Jesus, we want to go running meaning that we are already working for Him, and we just meet Him without taking a pause. ♡

Have you ever wished your personality was more like someone else's? Maybe you are shy and quiet and wish you could be more outgoing. Maybe you are loud and funny and wish you could be seen as serious and trustworthy. I bet most of us have wished that some part of our personality was different.

Consider this statement:

Our personalities are not for us; they are for God.

That statement made me think. God made us. He chose us. He wants to use us for His kingdom. God can use every single personality for His glory.

Moses was not a speaker, and God chose him.
Mary was meek, and God used her.
Peter was arrogant, and God used him.

Rather than wishing to have different personality traits, what if we take who we are to God and say, "Use me." He needs our faith and obedience. He will do the rest. ♡

A good friend recently commented that everyone needs to make room for the luxury of a pause. Think about it for a moment.

We are all moving in different paths each day as we balance life and its demands. Do you ever just stop to breathe? Do you pause to simply be thankful for the moment? Do you bask in the day that the Lord has made?

> "This is the day that the Lord has made; let us rejoice and
> be glad in it."
>
> Psalm 118:24 ESV

> "Be still and know that I am God."
>
> Psalm 46:10 ESV

The luxury of a pause needs to be taken more often. Pause to pray, pause to reflect, pause to rest. God loves us and creates us for His purpose. It is sometimes in those pauses that we can find that real purpose. ♡

Do you ever have troubles? I think all of us can relate. Troubles ebb and flow in our lives; the question is how do we deal with them? What does God say to do with our troubles?

**Get started.** We are to trust God and seek His direction and then be obedient.

> "Behold, God is my salvation; I will trust, and will not be afraid; for the Lord God is my strength and my song, and he has become my salvation."
>
> Isaiah 12:2 ESV

**Don't quit.** Troubles are hard and sometimes can seem overwhelming. God says not to quit. He is with us.

> "And we know that for those who love God all things work together for good, for those who are called according to his purpose."
>
> Romans 8:28 ESV

**Believe in God.** He has got this. He wasn't surprised by it, and He won't leave you.

> "Do not be anxious about anything, but in everything by prayer and supplication with thanksgiving let your requests be made known to God. And the peace of God, which surpasses all understanding, will guard your hearts and your minds in Christ Jesus."
>
> Philippians 4:6-7 ESV

**Take courage.**

> "Be strong and courageous. Do not fear or be in dread of them, for it is the Lord your God who goes with you. He will not leave you or forsake you."
>
> Deuteronomy 31:6 ESV

**Serve Him.**

> "If anyone serves me, he must follow me; and where I am, there will my servant be also. If anyone serves me, the Father will honor him."
>
> John 12:26 ESV

God didn't promise us a life free of trouble, but He does promise to walk with us through every step if we will invite Him. ♡

• • •

## Troubles ebb and flow...What do we do when they come?

Have you ever had a moment when you paused and smiled and thought to yourself, "God did that"?

There are those times when life just fits together, or problems resolve in ways that we just know that God intervened. Often those times have been prayerfully sought, and other times they seem to be unexpected surprises.

Do you think it is a coincidence that God provided roughly 365 times in the Bible that tell us not to fear? He knew that fear and doubt would plague our human minds and He speaks, "fear not" over and over and over again so much so that we could read a different verse about every day of the year.

God said it in the Old Testament.

> "It is the Lord who goes before you. He will be with you; he will not leave you or forsake you. Do not fear or be dismayed."
>
> Deuteronomy 31:8 ESV

Jesus said it in the New Testament.

> "Peace I leave with you; my peace I give to you. Not as the world gives do I give to you. Let not your hearts be troubled, neither let them be afraid."
>
> John 14:27 ESV

Now, will we embrace it? Fear is hard. Fear can affect all parts of our lives. It can paralyze us.

Or we can focus on God and claim His promises day after day to help combat the hold that fear may have on us. Today can be a great starting point. ♡

What is your exercise routine? Are you a daily energizer, a weekly mover, or a recliner holder?

Physical exercise is a weakness for me. I move all day, but it is not in a way that truly exercises my body. I don't make it a priority. Guilty.

What about our spiritual exercise? Huh? Is that a thing? Look with me in 1 Timothy:

> "... Rather train yourself for godliness; for while bodily training is of some value, godliness is of value in every way, as it holds promise for the present life and also for the life to come."
>
> 1 Timothy 4:7-8 ESV

Yep. God said it. What are we doing daily to grow our spiritual strength? What are we doing to plant our roots of faith deeper to help us when trouble comes our way? What are we doing to deepen our own understanding of God in order to be able to share with others?

As you consider exercise in the coming days, consider spiritual exercise, too. It has an eternal impact. ♡

If you hear the phrase "deep and wide," does a childhood tune start ringing in your head?

I read a profound statement recently. A Christian said that our faith needed to be deep rather than shallow. When a non-believer asked why, the wise woman replied, "When our faith is shallow, it is hard for us to truly love and serve others the way God loves and serves. When our faith is deep, then we have gone through experiences that have tested our faith, and we can love and serve others from a far richer perspective." Whew! That is deep.

Think about it. Jesus's faith was tried. He had sorrows. He had betrayal, abuse, beatings, and death. You may be walking in sorrow now. All of us will walk in it again if we live long enough. The question is are we allowing the path of sorrow to deepen our faith? Or is it driving a wedge? Only we can answer that question as individuals. ♡

Have you ever heard the old saying about "getting your cart ahead of your horse?" I loved the many "sayings" that my family introduced to me throughout childhood. I have been guilty of this one more often than I would like to admit, especially when it comes to God.

Look at this verse in Acts:

> "And when they had prayed, the place in which they were gathered together was shaken, and they were all filled with the Holy Spirit and continued to speak the word of God with boldness."
>
> Acts 4:31 ESV

Did you notice that? AFTER they prayed, they spoke the Word of God boldly. They didn't just charge into a conversation and start spewing their thoughts. They prayed *first*, they focused *first*, they sought God *first*.

Look at this verse in Jeremiah:

> "Call to me and I will answer you and will tell you great and hidden things that you have not known."
>
> Jeremiah 33:3 ESV

I sometimes must lead difficult conversations. It isn't fun. I have found time and time again that those conversations go so much better when I spend time in prayer before them. I ask God to go before and open hearts and minds, and I pray for His direction in my words and reactions.

If you are called to wade into a difficult conversation, pray first. If you can share your faith, whisper a prayer first. If you find yourself in a scary situation, pray and then speak. God made you. God loves you. God is with you. ♡

Do you ever worry about tomorrow? Do you worry about things that may not even happen? I am guilty.

I worry about the future. I worry about my children, my grandchildren. Sound familiar?

What does God say?

> "And of Asher he said, 'Most blessed of sons be Asher; let him be the favorite of his brothers and let him dip his foot in oil. Your bars shall be iron and bronze, and as your days, so shall your strength be'."
>
> Deuteronomy 33:24-25 ESV

Notice the last part of this verse: "and as your days, so shall your strength be." God is saying He will provide you with the strength you need for **EACH** day *on that day*.

Look again.

> "Let us then with confidence draw near to the throne of grace, that we may receive mercy and find grace to help in time of need."
>
> Hebrews 4:16 ESV

Look at this verse: "and find grace to help in the time of need." Again, God will provide us with the strength we need WHEN we need it.

I heard a preacher share that we are not to try to face tomorrow's problems with today's strength. God will provide us with what we need when we need it. We are not to worry about tomorrow. We are to focus on today and live each day for Christ! ♡

Is trust hard for you? Are you able to extend blind trust, or are you one that requires trust to be earned?

What happens when trust is broken? Can you rebuild or do you simply walk away, forever?

I read a powerful statement this week. It made me stop; it made me think and reflect. See what it says to you:

"Be able to discern your Judas from your Peter. Peter had a bad day, Judas had a bad heart. Peter, you restore. Judas, you release."

Whew. Now that will preach. Yes, God says to love one another. He also says we are to use discernment to help us know each other.

> "And do not be conformed to this world, but be transformed by the renewing of your mind, that you may prove what is that good and acceptable and perfect will of God."
> Romans 12:2 ESV

> "Behold I send you out as sheep in the midst of wolves. Therefore, be wise as serpents and harmless as doves."
> Matthew 10: 16 ESV

Hmmm. God will help us discern our relations with other people and help us know what direction to take. Yes, He commands us to forgive, and He helps us discern. ♡

Have you ever heard the phrase "talk the talk, but can't walk the walk"? It is likely that we have all seen (or done) this over the years. We encounter a person who is quick to say all of the right things, but rarely is known to actually follow through and do them.

I wish I could say that hasn't been me, but that would not be truthful. There are many things in life that I know to do, eat better, exercise more, focus on positives, love people (especially the hard ones).

The question is do I "profess" the right behaviors, or do I "possess" them? Do I tell others (profess) what needs to be done or am I actually doing (possessing) them?

Consider this scripture:

"This is why I speak to them in parables, because seeing they do not see, and hearing they do not hear, nor do they understand.

> But blessed are your eyes, for they see, and your ears, for they hear."
> Matthew 13:13, 16 ESV

I don't want to be a professing Christian who only puts on the front with all of the right words; I want to be a Christian who has His Word deep in my heart and lives it daily. Will my walk be perfect? No. But I can certainly push toward that mark every day. ♡

When Spring is in the air, the fish are biting! (Or so it seems based on social media pics.) Have you ever been fishing? Have you ever been fishing from a boat?

Boats can drift. You could kick back with that trusty fishing pole and think that you aren't moving and wake up from a quick nap to find that you have moved quite far.

This is when the anchor becomes so very important. Even in a smallish pond, we can drop anchor and hold fast.

Did you know we have a spiritual anchor? No matter where we are in life, we have the promise of God to be with us.

> "We have this as a sure and steadfast anchor of the soul, a
> hope that enters into the inner place behind the curtain."
> Hebrews 6:19 ESV

There are many promises from God in the Bible. His promises are our anchor. He is with us, and He loves us. He will see us through. We just have to trust Him. ♡

Lord, Lord.

> "Why do you call me 'Lord, Lord,' and not do what I tell you?"
>
> Luke 6:46 ESV

Do you ever get a feeling that God is telling you to do something? This is called conviction. Sometimes, we are convicted of doing things that are difficult, and all we want to do is run away. However, when we run away, we are trying to compromise with God. We want the benefits of a relationship but when He asks us to obey Him, we are not willing to do the hard work. What area of your life is God convicting you to honor Him with? Are you running away from the conviction or are you truly saying, "Yes, Lord." ♡

When was the last time someone knocked on your door? Does a knock on your front door usually mean it is a guest (because family and friends just come on in the back door)?

Did you know Jesus tells us to knock as well?

> "Ask, and it will be given to you; seek, and you will find; knock, and it will be opened to you. For everyone who asks receives, and the one who seeks finds, and to the one who knocks it will be opened."
>
> Matthew 7:7-8 ESV

Did you know that God wants to be involved in our lives? I don't mean just a Sunday event; He wants to be part of our daily lives, even the small stuff. I cannot help but wonder how many times I have made decisions without asking Him, without knocking on His door and waiting to see His direction. I wonder what blessing I have missed because of my impatience and lack of focus.

As I have aged, I have become much less quick to act (or react), and I truly knock and seek and ask. Guess what??? He answers, and my life is better for it. I ask Him to open and close doors as He sees fit, and I must be willing to accept the closed ones and walk through the open ones.

Take time today to pray. Have a talk with Jesus. Ask Him to meet your needs. Seek His direction. Look for doors that open for you. Know that you are a welcome part of His family anytime, any day! ♡

Has anyone ever made you angry? Fire-breathing, foot-stomping, blood-pounding angry? What did you do? (Notice that I didn't ask what the person did; I asked what you did in reaction to the person.)

The Bible is full of examples of God's direction on how we should respond when we have been wronged. He says to forgive. Period. Whew. Easier said than done, right?

Look at this scripture in Matthew 18:

> "Then Peter came up and said to him, "Lord, how often will my brother sin against me, and I forgive him? As many as seven times?" Jesus said to him, "I do not say to you seven times, but seventy-seven times."
>
> Matthew 18:21-22 ESV

Did Jesus say 70 times 7? As in 490 times? Yep. He did. Think about it. How many times has God forgiven us? (Mine is probably in the tens of thousands.) Aren't we thankful that God doesn't keep count?

In all honesty, when we harbor the anger of unforgiveness, it is most often we that suffer. The anger festers and grows until it begins to steal our joy. This is a lesson I struggle with sometimes. There are some wrongs that just seem unforgivable, and they are unless we ask God for help.

> "But Jesus looked at them and said, "With man this is impossible, but with God all things are possible."
>
> Matthew 19:26 ESV

If you are struggling today with the bitterness of unforgiveness, share it with God. If anger and hatred are stealing your joy, ask God to be your partner toward overcoming it. We cannot change the past, but we can choose our reaction to it by seeking to find peace and joy with God. ♡

● ● ●

## Foot-stomping, Fire-breathing Mad...What Do You Do?

When was the last time you watched the sunrise? Was it from your car on the way to work or maybe from your tractor seat or even from your kitchen window? When was the last time you stopped to look up at the night sky? Have you ever lay in the grass and stopped to ponder the wonder of the stars and moon? (I know that for some of us it is difficult to get up once we get down, right?)

Have you ever considered that sometimes we are soooooo busy doing whatever it is that life tells us we need to be doing that we fail to ever pause and just *be*?

Look at Psalm 8:

> "When I look at your heavens, the work of your fingers, the moon and the stars, which you have set in place, what is man that you are mindful of him, and the son of man that you care for him?"
>
> Psalm 8:3-4 ESV

Sometimes we get caught up in thinking that every single thing we do is of utmost importance when we actually need to pause and just *be*. We need to revel in the glory of God and His creation. We need to remember the point of our existence is to know Him and worship Him. Make some time to just *be*. Slow down and focus on Him. ♡

What is your favorite fruit? I can be a fruit snob. I love a crisp, sweet apple or an almost green banana and I can devour multiples of those little tangerines that are so easy to peel! On the flip side, I absolutely do not like a soft apple, or a truly ripe banana and I cannot be bothered to fight with citrus that is hard to peel and eat. (I know. Strong opinions. Guilty.)

I wonder if God looks at my fruit and has the same pickiness. I am not talking about the fruit I eat; I mean the fruit I bear.

Look at this scripture:

> "I am the true vine, and my Father is the vinedresser. Every branch in me that does not bear fruit he takes away, and every branch that does bear fruit he prunes, that it may bear more fruit. Already you are clean because of the word that I have spoken to you. Abide in me, and I in you. As the branch cannot bear fruit by itself, unless it abides in the vine, neither can you, unless you abide in me."
>
> John 15:1-4 ESV

God wants us to live in such a way that we bear fruit for Him. Each day we live is an opportunity for us to share God with others through our words and actions.

In Galatians it is very clear what God wants us to bear.

> "But the fruit of the Spirit is love, joy, peace, patience, kindness, goodness, faithfulness, gentleness, self-control; against such things there is no law."
>
> Galatians 5:22-23 ESV

Whew! I know that each of these traits is great, but I cannot say that they are all easy for me. What about you? There is room for some pruning in my life. ♡

# Nanny's Fried Okra and Tomatoes

3-4 cups of fried okra (extra done)
1 small tomato
⅓ cup sugar
3 tbsp oil

Heat the oil to sizzling at medium heat. (You can use some of the oil left over from frying the okra). Dice the tomato into small pieces and toss into the oil. Add the sugar. As the juice begins to caramelize (thicken and bubble), toss in the fried okra. Keep adding and stirring until all of the okra is tossed in the tomato mixture. Cook for about 2-3 minutes (until liquid is absorbed) and remove from heat.

● ● ●

This is a well-loved dish from my mother-in-law. I have no idea if it originated with her or if she acquired it, but we LOVE it and often requested it in her kitchen! I must admit that it can be tricky, and I don't always nail it! Two big tips are to truly overcook the okra when frying it and to choose a small tomato. If the tomato is too large, there will be too much juice and the okra will get soggy.

## Nanny's Fried Okra and Tomato

Do you ever worry about your appearance? Do you stress over what to wear to an event or what new hairstyle to choose?

Most of us innately want to look our best. Our society adds extra pressure through television and magazines and the power of social media. Thanks to such things as filters, we can shave age and weight rather quickly.

The problem is that those filters aren't real, and truthfully, our outer looks only go skin deep. What about our hearts? What kind of people are we from the inside?

Samuel was sent by God to the house of Jesse to anoint the future king. God told Samuel that He would direct him about which son had been chosen. Look at the scripture below:

> "But the Lord said to Samuel, 'Do not look on his appearance or on the height of his stature, because I have rejected him. For the Lord sees not as man sees: man looks on the outward appearance, but the Lord looks on the heart'."
>
> 1 Samuel 16:7 ESV

Do you see that? God is much more concerned about the heart. Samuel, a person who loved God greatly, even made the mistake of looking for the person who had a great outer appearance. God had to redirect his assumptions and remind Samuel about what is important to God.

Our hearts are much more important to Him because that is where He resides. ♡

Have you ever heard the phrase "Not today, Satan!"? Maybe you have even used it. This phrase comes to mind when we have an unexpected flat tire or a broken washing machine or a sassy child, or maybe all these things. We tend to feel like the devil is after us when life is falling apart.

What if... what if the devil is more cunning than this? What if sometimes the devil is in our plenty? What if the devil seeks to use the financial blessings, we receive to draw us away from our dependence on God? What if our new love interest is used to pull our focus away from God? We must be vigilant to protect our relationship with Christ. The devil will use whatever is needed to try to pull us away; He may even try to use our blessings for distraction.

I have been reading about King Hezekiah in II Kings and II Chronicles and saw this happen. Hezekiah was picked by God to lead, and he did so well for a long time. And then he didn't. He let the devil slide in and use his success against him. We must not be deceived; we must be thoughtful to check ourselves often to be sure that God is the center of our lives. ♡

Who are your five? Some experts say that we tend to become a mix of the five people with whom we are closest.

Who are the five people who influence you most? What traits from each have worn off on you?

Do you agree that it is important to be thoughtful when choosing who is part of your inner circle? Jesus did. He chose twelve. He knew He would have roughly three years of ministry to pour into these disciples. He chose fishermen, a doctor, a tax collector, siblings, strangers. Jesus chose a variety. What united them was a desire to learn and grow and follow. Were they perfect? No. They doubted, they slept on the job, and one even turned traitor.

Jesus poured into them all. He loved them, corrected them, and grew them. Are you growing as a result of the people who surround you? Are you pouring into those people so they can grow? Are you collectively growing the Kingdom of God by sharing Christ with others? ♡

"Joshua fought the battle of Jericho, Jericho, Jericho...." Do you remember this song from childhood? (You are welcome that it will now be on repeat in your head today.)

I have always loved the story of the falling of the walls of Jericho. As a child, it seemed almost like the story of a superhero that horns and shouts could bring down those massive walls. (The story is in Joshua 6.)

As I was reading through it again this week, I couldn't help but consider how much faith was required. Fact 1: that the people respected and trusted Joshua enough to follow such unusual directions: faith. Fact 2: that the soldiers and priests and others marched around an entire city in silence: faith. Fact 3: that the process was repeated for seven entire days: faith. Fact: that the seventh day required seven full trips around the city rather than just once: faith.

> "But Joshua commanded the people, 'You shall not shout
> or make your voice heard, neither shall any word go out
> of your mouth, until the day I tell you to shout. Then you
> shall shout'."
>
> Joshua 6:10 ESV

Can you see the scenario today? I can imagine doubt, dissension, distraction, and desertion. Maybe Joshua experienced those things, too. It doesn't say in the scripture; however, it does clearly give direction from God and those walls did come tumbling down. That means that there was obedience and faith.

Is there something in your life today in which God is calling for obedience? Is He calling for you to have faith? Trust Him. ♡

Do you watch action movies or maybe read action novels? What are heroes like? How would you describe them? Are they muscular and strong? Are they dressed to make your heart throb? Do they wield weapons like an expert? Do they drive amazing vehicles performing death-defying stunts? Let's take a moment to talk about the greatest hero of all time.

You may have seen posts on social media where people are hanging simple palm fronds on their doors and wondered why. Christians are celebrating Palm Sunday and, again, you may think, "Why a palm? It isn't the prettiest of plants. It doesn't have a fragrance. It isn't very colorful among all of these glorious spring flowers. Why a palm?" It all has to do with that unlikely hero. Join me in Matthew 21:

> "Now when they drew near to Jerusalem and came to Bethphage, to the Mount of Olives, then Jesus sent two disciples, saying to them, "Go into the village in front of you, and immediately you will find a donkey tied, and a colt with her. Untie them and bring them to me. If anyone says anything to you, you shall say, 'The Lord needs them,' and he will send them at once." This took place to fulfill what was spoken by the prophet, saying, "Say to the daughter of Zion, 'Behold, your king is coming to you, humble, and mounted on a donkey, on a colt, the foal of a beast of burden'." Matthew 21:1-4 ESV

Now He is ready to make a triumphant entry down into Jerusalem and what will He use? A donkey. Huh? The Son of God, our Savior, the hero who is going to willingly give His LIFE in a most painful and humiliating way, is going to ride in on a donkey?? Why not a stallion? Wouldn't that be more fitting for who Jesus is? Nah. You see, our God is unique. He doesn't fit the mold of society, not then and not now. Our God is for ALL and Jesus shows us His humility and approachability and availability again and again.... even though He is the King of kings.)

> 6 "The disciples went and did as Jesus had directed them. They brought the donkey and the colt and put on them

their cloaks, and he sat on them. Most of the crowd spread their cloaks on the road, and others cut branches from the trees and spread them on the road. And the crowds that went before him and that followed him were shouting, "Hosanna to the Son of David! Blessed is he who comes in the name of the Lord! Hosanna in the highest!"

Matthew 21:6-9 ESV

(Have you ever attended a parade? Were there bright lights and music? Maybe there were ornate floats and marching bands? Again, our Jesus is unique. These people didn't come for fun; they came to WORSHIP. They laid down their coats, and they placed cut palms on the ground in HONOR of who He is and what He was doing and going to do for them. This is where we get Palm Sunday.)

Let's focus on Jesus. Go take a walk and look for a palmetto bush or a palm tree along our paths and pause and lift our hands and pray in celebration for all Jesus has and will do for us! ♡

Have you ever been thankful for a second chance? Goodness, I have. I have celebrated many anniversaries of second chances.

Aren't you thankful that God understands that none of us are perfect?

Consider Jonah: it took time in the belly of a big fish and then sweating under a leafless tree to get him in the right direction.

Consider Peter: it took hearing the rooster crow before he could truly step into his path.

Consider Saul: it took a blinding-light "God" encounter on Damascus Road and a conversation with Ananias to cause his about-face.

While we may not be guaranteed tomorrow, I am so very thankful that God allows us opportunities to learn and grow in today. ♡

"God don't like ugly." While not grammatically correct, this statement has been used in our extended family as a note of humor over the years when we can see that God is not rewarding bad behavior. I can think of a few times that some family member has quietly uttered it, and the rest of us nearby have struggled to keep a straight face.

God does sometimes seem to have a sense of humor in how he redirects our bad behaviors. He can also be direct and firm and, as we southerners say, "yank our chains" as needed, too.

We need to remember this when we have been wronged and are considering revenge. God is clear that we can trust Him to handle it.

> "Beloved, never avenge yourselves, but leave it to the wrath of God, for it is written, 'Vengeance is mine, I will repay, says the Lord'."
>
> Romans 12:19 ESV

Not only does God tell us to let Him take care of vengeance, but He also tells us to embrace the old "kill them with kindness" adage.

> "To the contrary, 'If your enemy is hungry, feed him; if he is thirsty, give him something to drink; for by so doing, you will heap burning coals on his head'."
>
> Romans 12:20 ESV

This can be a tough one for a lot of us. It is easy to love someone who loves us, but it is tough to love someone who has wronged us. God says to do it anyway.

> "Do not be overcome by evil but overcome evil with good."
>
> Romans 12:21 ESV

Be encouraged today that you are not alone, and that God sees and knows all. God's timing is perfect, and He loves us. He's got us. ♡

● ● ●

## God Don't Like Ugly

"Mirror, mirror on the wall…"

This is a saying from a children's movie from my childhood. Did you know that God mentions something about "looking in the mirror" as well?

Look with me in James 1:

> "But be doers of the word, and not hearers only, deceiving yourselves. For if anyone is a hearer of the word and not a doer, he is like a man who looks intently at his natural face in a mirror. For he looks at himself and goes away and at once forgets what he was like."
>
> James 1:22-24 ESV

I am pretty sure if any of us look in the mirror and see a piece of food between our teeth or a smudge on our face, we are going to fix the blemish.

Are we as concerned when God shows us an area of our lives in which there is a dirty spot? Do we hear what God says to do and then ignore it?

Living our lives can be tough. The closer we grow to God, the more He teaches us things about ourselves. Sometimes He shows us things that we need to release, steps we need to take. Let's be doers today! Let's follow His lead. ♡

When was the last time you received an act of kindness? Better yet, when was the last time you provided an act of kindness?

I was reminded of the importance of these actions. Typical of my usual gracefulness, I had a tumble that resulted in a good dose of pain, and some follow up tests. Thankfully, all was well, and I was no worse for the wear. Enough of that; let's focus on the blessings. Folks at my workplace immediately jumped into action and gave of themselves in a myriad of ways. Medical folks demonstrated servant hearts in true southern hospitality. Friends and family responded with genuine love and concern.

Amid my clumsy embarrassment, my heart smiled. Look at this verse:

> "And walk in love, as Christ loved us and gave himself up
> for us, a fragrant offering and sacrifice to God."
>
> Ephesians 5:2 ESV

I experienced this verse in so many ways. I was humbled. I want to be a better neighbor who shows genuine, Christ-filled love to others. I am looking for those opportunities today. Don't you want to join me? ♡

Have you ever met someone who "rides on someone's coattails"? I am not sure where that saying originated, but it is interesting to sit back, and watch folks try to take credit for the work of others.

That may stir some ire in you as you read this. Maybe you have experienced this circumstance before. I want us to pause and consider it from a different view, a faithful view.

How deep is your own faith? Are you a walking, talking Christian in your daily life? Is Christ in every day? Do you seek to deepen that faith, or are you riding someone's coattails? Are you counting on the faith of your parents to make your way to Heaven? Are you seeking the prayers of your grandparents or friends to intercede for you? Are you hoping the faith of your spouse will cover you, too?

Look at what the scripture says:

> "Bear fruit in keeping with repentance. And do not presume to say to yourselves, 'We have Abraham as our father,' for I tell you, God is able from these stones to raise up children for Abraham. Even now the axe is laid to the root of the trees. Every tree therefore that does not bear good fruit is cut down and thrown into the fire."
>
> Matthew 3:8-10 ESV

Step. On. Toes. God is clear that our faith is our own. Our choices are our own. Faith is not a family discount or a two for one; it is an individual choice. Where is our faith today? Are we bearing fruit ♡

Are you anxious? Maybe afraid? Maybe worried about the future? Human nature lets these kinds of stresses slip into our hearts and often steal our joy.

Thankfully, God knew this was going to be a struggle for us, so He sent LOTS of verses to provide us comfort and courage. I want to share some of them with you today. Read them. Pray them. Write them somewhere you can see them often. Our God is never surprised at the events of our lives, and He promises to be right beside us for every step. (He will even guide those steps if we will allow Him.) ♡

> "Peace I leave with you; My peace I give to you. Not as the world gives do I give to you. Let not your hearts be troubled, neither let them be afraid."
>
> John 14:27 ESV

> "Cast all your cares(anxieties) on him, because he cares about you."
>
> 1 Peter 5:7 ESV

> "Therefore, do not be anxious about tomorrow, for tomorrow will be anxious for itself. Sufficient for the day is its own trouble."
>
> Matthew 6:34 ESV

> "Let your gentleness be known to everyone. The Lord is at hand. Do not be anxious about anything, but in everything, by prayer and supplication with thanksgiving let your requests be made known to God. And the peace of God, which surpasses all understanding, will guard your hearts and minds in Christ Jesus."
>
> Philippians 4:5-7

"That nose is turned so far in the air that a person may drown if it rains!" Have you ever met someone who fits this description?

Better question: have you ever been that person? As a Christian?

I read the book of Jonah this week. (Quick review: God tells Jonah to go to Nineveh to deliver God's message. Jonah doesn't want to go, so he skips town on a boat. A storm comes, and Jonah is swallowed by a fish. The fish spits Jonah out. Jonah goes to Nineveh and the people repent. Because he needs shade, Jonah pouts. God provides a tree. A worm comes and eats the leaves, so Jonah pouts again). I considered a new point that had never really stood out to me before. I guess I was always more caught up in the whole "swallowed and spit out by a fish" thing.

Think through this with me. Jonah was a prophet. God chose him to deliver a message that Nineveh would be destroyed unless they repent. Get this: God wanted them to have a chance to repent and be spared, but Jonah didn't want them to have the chance. Jonah had his nose turned up regarding these people. He procrastinated, and he tried to avoid God's direction. (Have we ever been guilty?)

After Jonah is swallowed by the fish and ponders for three days, he is spit out and runs to tell Nineveh. Guess what? Those people did EXACTLY what God asked. They repented and sought God. And guess what? Jonah was frustrated. He didn't think they were sincere, and he didn't think they deserved another chance. His nose is turned up again. (Has this ever been us in our daily walks?)

Here is what spoke to me. Jonah, a Christian, a prophet, was the only person not on board with God's plan. Jonah thought his opinion was better than God's. If we are honest, we have all likely been Jonah at some point. I am guilty. I am convicted.

God sees the big picture. He is the author of the Master Plan. It isn't for us to judge His plan. We are to seek Him and follow His direction. Not our will, but His will be done. ♡

•   •   •

## Noses in the Air

In the spirit of Easter and everything it represents, these simple words pack powerful meaning anytime throughout the year.

It is Friday; Sunday is coming.

He was betrayed.
He had supper.
He went to pray.
He was arrested.
He was denied.
He was beaten.
He was nailed.
He was mocked.
He was pierced.
He was completely innocent.
He died for you and for me.
Sunday is coming. ♡

Did you ever have any "play" money as a child and wish that it was real? I used to imagine the great toys I could purchase if only that money was real.

I have been told several times that banks have a unique way of teaching tellers how to discern real money from counterfeit. The workers are taught to spot what is real. They learn what sets real money apart. They know it by look and touch. Their focus is always on the real thing. It then becomes easier to spot what is counterfeit.

Did you know that Jesus gave similar biblical advice? In Matthew 24, Jesus spoke to His disciples about times that would come (and those that haven't come yet).

> "Then if anyone says to you, 'Look, here is the Christ!' or 'There he is!' do not believe it. For false christs and false prophets will arise and perform great signs and wonders, so as to lead astray, if possible, even the elect."
> Matthew 24:23-24 ESV

Go read the whole chapter. It is both interesting and unsettling. There are going to be hard days in the future; some events could even be confusing, misleading. We must know the REAL one. We must know Him personally in our hearts so that we can discern real from counterfeit. We need to know His word and commit it to our hearts and minds so we can be prepared. We must know Jesus. ♡

Have you ever been caught "off guard"? Maybe someone told you something and it caught you "off guard," or maybe someone you love did something very uncharacteristic and it caught you "off guard." I bet we have all been there at least once. (Or quite often.)

God gave us clear direction about our faith. We are to be ON guard, and we are to be clear about our beliefs.

> "Be on guard. Stand firm in the faith. Be courageous. Be strong."
>
> 1 Corinthians 16:13 NLT

Paul is speaking to the Church of Corinth here, but God is speaking to us today. We are to be firm in our faith. Be courageous. Be strong. Sounds great, right?

So how do we do this? Prayer and His Word help me. Talking about Christ with fellow believers helps me. Listening to worship music helps me. What about you?

Seek your heart today. What draws you closer to Christ and helps you stand stronger on your faith in Him? Make this a priority. Let's invest in our faith so that we are ready to stand no matter what may come our way. ♡

What is your favorite tool? A hammer, a spade, a screwdriver, a rake? Have you noticed that tools just don't seem to be as sturdy as they once were? I have noticed that even the metal sometimes seems weaker. It doesn't seem up to the toughest of jobs.

What about us? Look at this scripture in Proverbs 27:

> "Iron sharpens iron, and one man sharpens another."
> Proverbs 27:17 ESV

Iron is tough. Iron on iron can sharpen. God seems to be using this as an analogy that Christians can be like iron; we can sharpen each other. We can hold each other accountable. We can grow each other in our Christian walks. We can support each other.

Are we? Are we doing this for each other? Are we loving each other enough to wade into deeper conversations? Are we lovingly confronting the tough issues that could pull us apart?

Avoidance is much easier, but it isn't God's way. He knows we aren't perfect. He knows we make mistakes. He wants us to "sharpen" each other. God wants us to forge strong relationships as Christians so we can stand firmly united in Him. ♡

Have you ever heard a statement like this: "Who do you think you are? The queen of Sheba"? This was a somewhat popular phrase I heard people use during my childhood. (My daddy may have even directed it to me on occasions when I might have been a tad lazy.)

I always wondered who the actual queen of Sheba was and where did folks come up with this saying. Join me in 1 Kings:10:

> "Now when the queen of Sheba heard of the fame of Solomon concerning the name of the Lord, she came to test him with hard questions."
>
> 1 Kings 10:1 ESV

> "And she said to the king, 'The report was true that I heard in my own land of your words and of your wisdom, but I did not believe the reports until I came, and my own eyes had seen it. And behold, the half was not told me. Your wisdom and prosperity surpass the report that I heard'."
>
> 1 Kings 10:6-7 ESV

So she really was a person, a person from the Bible, a woman of wealth and power, a pretty uncommon combination in the Old Testament. It sounds like she was a woman of action. She had heard of King Solomon's great wisdom, so she loaded up her entourage and journeyed to his kingdom to see what it was all about.

If you go back to the early years of Solomon's reign (I Kings 3), you will see that he specifically asked God for wisdom, and this wisdom comes from God. It isn't Solomon's innate trait but rather a gift from God.

Our blessings come from God. Understand this: Even amid blessings, even when we have favor from God, we CAN fall into sin. King Solomon had been blessed immensely. He had the ability to discern and solve problems through the wisdom God gave him. He had financial wealth and was chosen to rebuild the temple for the Ark of the Covenant.

HOWEVER, he became too confident, arrogant, comfortable. He built himself a palace that far outsized the temple. He eventually began to build statues of other gods for the people he led. He took his eyes off God and lost his focus. He forgot the One who gave him his blessings. (Much like his daddy, King David, and his predecessor, King Saul.)

Do you notice the theme? Even folks who walk close with God, who have experienced His amazing power and blessings, CAN veer off the path that God wants for us. We must be intentional and seek His face and cling to Him to avoid the distractions the devil will put in our paths. ♡

● ● ●

## The Queen of Sheba...

One of my favorite old hymns is "Standing on the Solid Rock." It has pep and encouragement in real life situations!

"I'm standing on the rock of ages;
Safe from every storm that rages;
Rich, but not from Satan's wages.
I'm standing on the solid rock."

Did you know that Jesus used a similar "rock" analogy about the way we are to live? Read with me in Luke 6:

> "Everyone who comes to me and hears my words and does them, I will show you what he is like: he is like a man building a house, who dug deep and laid the foundation on the rock. And when a flood arose, the stream broke against that house and could not shake it, because it had been well built. But the one who hears and does not do them is like a man who built a house on the ground without a foundation. When the stream broke against it, immediately it fell, and the ruin of that house was great."
>
> Luke 6:47-49 ESV

Do you see what I see? Hearing is not enough. We are to be doers. We are to live what God's Word tells us. That doesn't mean just our actions in public. Jesus is also speaking about our time in prayer and in scripture. Our faith roots grow deep through action. It is when those roots run deep that we can stand the storms of life more firmly because our roots are wrapped around the Rock—God. I frankly don't like the storms that come, and I cannot imagine weathering one of them without Him. ♡

Did you know that sandpaper comes in various grades of grit? Some of it would peel your hide in a swipe, and others would cause a mere scuff.

Did you know there are "sandpaper" people in our world? Yep. There are. These are folks who just rub us the wrong way. They tend to come in varying grades of grit as well. Some just get on our nerves a tad while others drive us completely bonkers. Can you relate? It is ok to confess.

Here is a nugget to ponder. Did you know that the lower the number of grit on the paper the harsher it is? The higher the number of grit, the finer the sandpaper. I kind of relate to that a bit. When I was younger my patience was shorter and my grace toward others was limited. As a result, I let those sandpaper people really bother me. I have found that the older I get, the years must be breaking down that grit and causing those sandpaper people to not bother me nearly so much.

Or could it be that I have allowed God to embed deeper into my soul and spread into more areas of my daily life? Could it be that because God has shown so very much forgiveness and grace to me that I now understand why it is important to do the same for others?

There is a note on my desk to help me keep this focus. It reads: "Lord, please help me to love whomever you place in front of me today." This task isn't always easy and some days those sandpaper folks still scrape my skin, but my response is better than it has been and continues to improve with God's help. ♡

Are you one of those people who likes to hear rain on the roof? Maybe you enjoy a summer afternoon thunderstorm.

I sometimes enjoy these, too, but I don't like the thunderstorms of life. I don't like being tossed about in the wind and lightning of life's storms. I don't like the lack of control and fear of what is next. Can you relate?

Peter could, too. Look in Matthew 14:

"But immediately Jesus spoke to them, saying, 'Take heart; it is I. Do not be afraid'."

> And Peter answered him, "Lord, if it is you, command me to come to you on the water." He said, "Come." So Peter got out of the boat and walked on the water and came to Jesus. But when he saw the wind, he was afraid, and beginning to sink he cried out, "Lord, save me." Jesus immediately reached out his hand and took hold of him, saying to him, "O you of little faith, why did you doubt?" And when they got into the boat, the wind ceased. And those in the boat worshiped him, saying, "Truly you are the Son of God."
>
> Matthew 14: 27-33 ESV

I struggle with faith sometimes, too. It comforts me to know that even Peter, who was face-to-face with Jesus, could be afraid and have doubts. Peter cried out, "Lord, save me!" Maybe you have a situation today that is frightening and challenging your faith. Seek out Jesus, and He will be there. In the words of a favorite song, "He's as close as the mention of His name!" ♡

Do you vote? Do you exercise your right to vote? Did you know there is a public record of who voted in the elections? Don't misunderstand me - there is no record of who you voted for, just a record of if you actually cast any votes.

There will be a record of your name at another time. God references it in His Word.

> "But nothing unclean will ever enter it, nor anyone who does what is detestable or false, but only those who are written in the Lamb's book of life."
>
> Revelation 21:27 ESV

God is referencing Heaven. We cannot enter if our names are not there. We must choose God, choose His salvation, accept His Grace and Mercy, for our names to be there.

> "Not everyone who says to me, 'Lord, Lord,' will enter the kingdom of heaven, but the one who does the will of my Father who is in heaven."
>
> Matthew 7:21 ESV

Jesus was clear that simply being aware of Him is not enough. We are to live for Him; we are to CHOOSE Him. The choice is yours. ♡

*Peace.* It is defined as "a quiet and calm state of mind; agreement and harmony among people."

In our current world, peace can seem elusive, difficult to find. From the roller coaster of the pandemic to the news of war to simple everyday struggles, fear can seem much closer than peace. What does God say about fear?

> "For I, the Lord your God, hold your right hand; it is I who say to you, "Fear not, I am the one who helps you.""
>
> Isaiah 41:13 ESV

> "Let us then with confidence draw near to the throne of grace, that we may receive mercy and find grace to help in time of need."
>
> Hebrews 4:16 ESV

There is a Peace that passes all understanding. His name is Jesus.

> "And the peace of God, which surpasses all understanding, will guard your hearts and your minds in Christ Jesus."
>
> Philippians 4:7 ESV

In the words of Jesus himself,

> "I have said these things to you, that in me you may have peace. In the world you will have tribulation. But take heart; I have overcome the world."
>
> John 16:33 ESV

If fear is stealing your joy today, meditate on these promises. Let them soak into your hearts and know that God is with us. ♡

Have you ever been to a carnival and had to purchase tokens to be able to ride the attractions? Have you ever taken children to a location that requires tokens? Have mercy those little tickets can add up quickly!!!

The word token implies a small amount: a "token" of appreciation, a small gift meant to convey thanks, a "token" to ride the Ferris wheel, a small fee for a few minutes of fun.

Consider this: What have we given Jesus lately? Is He getting our full focus or is He getting a "token" of our attention?

Look with me in scripture:

> "And he called his disciples to him and said to them, 'Truly, I say to you, this poor widow has put in more than all those who are contributing to the offering box. For they all contributed out of their abundance, but she out of her poverty has put in everything she had, all she had to live on'."
>
> Mark 12:43-44 ESV

Ouch. I am guilty. I must admit that I am often the "they" more than the widow. Whether it is time, money, commitment, faith or some other facet, I am sometimes guilty of giving a token rather than a full commitment.

What about you? Can we all learn a lesson from this cheerful giver today?

# Granny Bonnie's Turkey Dressing

| | |
|---|---|
| 1 turkey (14-18 lbs) | 5 cups water |
| 1 stick butter | |
| | |
| 2 c cornmeal | ⅓ c oil |
| ⅔ c flour | 1 large box saltines |
| 2 eggs | 1 loaf sliced bread |
| Milk (enough to mix cornbread | 4 c water |
| 1 c celery | 10-12 bouillon cubes |
| 1 c onion | 10 boiled eggs |

Place the THAWED turkey in a large roaster. Rub softened butter on turkey and sprinkle with salt. Pour water into the roaster. Cover with aluminum foil and bake at 350°°until done. (Most turkeys have a red tag that "pops" up when done. This will take several hours.)

Once the turkey is done and cooling, place a 9x9x2 pan (or a cast iron frying pan) with the ⅓ cup of oil into the 350° oven to heat. While the oil is getting hot, mix the cornmeal and flour together and then add the milk and eggs and stir until thick cake batter consistency. Add the celery and onions. (My gang is NOT a fan of celery and onions, so I puree them. This allows the amazing flavor, but no eye shall see them. :) Pull the hot oil out of the oven and pour into the cornbread mixture. Stir and pour the batter into the hot pan. Place back into the 350° oven and bake until springy to the touch. (Don't over bake it.)

While the cornbread is baking, crush the saltines and add to a large baking pan (like a roaster). Pinch the bread into small pieces and add to the saltines. Mix the water and bouillon cubes in a pot on the stove and bring to a boil to dissolve the cubes. Pour this hot mixture into the saltine and bread mixture and stir. Crumble the hot cornbread into this mixture and add broth from the turkey and mix until soft. (Always mix softer than you prefer because it will "set up" during baking.) Add the 10 chopped boiled eggs. If the mixture is too stiff, add more hot water in small quantities until you get the consistency you desire. (My mixture is on the verge of soupy. It becomes more solid, but still soft during baking. We DON'T like stiff dressing.)

Put this heavy roaster into a 400° oven and bake until golden brown on top. (Technically, it is all done before entering the oven, so I definitely lick that spoon!)

● ● ●

This is a two-video event. LOL! This recipe came from my Granny Bonnie and it is well-loved by MANY people. Rarely are there any leftovers! Come join me as I prepare for Thanksgiving.

## Granny Bonnie's Dressing Part 1

## Granny Bonnie's Dressing Part 2

Finish this verse: "Greater love hath no man..."

Were you able to finish it in your head? It is found in John 15:13. It is a verse I have grappled with at times.

> "Greater love hath no man than this, that a man lay down his life for his friends."
>
> John 15:13 KJV

Don't get me wrong: I do want to help my friends, but dying for them? That causes a deep gulp. Yet Jesus is clearly speaking here; it is even in red letters in my Bible.

I read something this weekend that made me think. What if Jesus wasn't necessarily referring to actual death (although that is the sacrifice that He made for us)? What if He means that we die to "self" by sacrificing for our friends? Think about this.

What if he means you do without a new outfit or a fancy dinner in order to help a friend who is struggling financially? What if He means that you miss watching a sporting event because you load up your mower and go cut grass for a sick friend? What if He means that you miss out on some quiet time at home in order to go visit with a person who is lonely?

What if "laying down my life" is not one singular grandiose act, but rather hundreds or thousands of small or large sacrifices to show His love to others? ♡

How often do you mop the floor? (My answer: not as often as I should.) Have you ever mopped really well only to find that there are spots that you missed? I have learned to pause and take a step back each time I mop a section. This step back helps me see the floor from a different perspective, and I can see the places I have missed.

Isn't life the same way? Don't we often get caught up in the daily (or hourly) drama and feel our stress levels soar? However, when we can step away for a moment and take a breath, we look back and see everything from a different perspective.

Look at this scripture:

> "When I think on my ways, I turn my feet to your testimonies;
> I hasten and do not delay to keep your commandments."
> Psalm 119:59-60 ESV

Sometimes we need to step away, think, and refocus on God. How would He handle this situation? What would He want us to do? Never do I mop without having to step back and check myself; isn't life more important than my floor? ♡

Have you ever been to a "meet and greet"? There is something about the excitement of coming together to cheer on groups as they march past.

Palm Sunday marks the remembrance of a special parade. Jesus entered Jerusalem while riding on a donkey. Bystanders were so excited about His entrance that they cut palm fronds and tossed them into the ground ahead of him. (Seems kinda like His own red carpet, right?)

> "The next day the large crowd that had come to the feast heard that Jesus was coming to Jerusalem. So, they took branches of palm trees and went out to meet him, crying out, "Hosanna! Blessed is he who comes in the name of the Lord, even the King of Israel!""
>
> John 12:12-13 ESV

While one group of people was very excited to welcome Jesus, another group was already plotting to get rid of Him. Jesus was becoming too popular; He was teaching people His Father's plan (and this plan didn't align with what the religious leaders wanted).

I can't help but wonder what Jesus was thinking as He rode into town. He knew where He was headed. He knew His week would end on a cross and in a tomb. Jesus was headed to be crucified for you and me, to cover our sins. The only sinless person to ever walk on earth was about to take on the sins of the world.

As you go through this week, take time to consider the road to the cross. Remember that Jesus loves you. ♡

"Too many offer God prayers with claw marks all over them."

I read this quote recently and I chuckled because I am guilty. Are you?

Do you pray for God to help you and then hold onto that issue and try to fix it yourself or worry and stew over it? God says for us to bring our burdens to Him.

> "Do not be anxious about anything, but in everything by prayer and supplication with thanksgiving let your requests be made known to God. And the peace of God, which surpasses all understanding, will guard your hearts and your minds in Christ Jesus."
>
> Philippians 4:6-7 ESV

Why is this so hard for us? Why do we struggle with truly laying our burdens at Jesus's feet and leaving them there?

A young boy in our church was headed to major surgery. He told his mama that he wasn't scared because he and his class prayed about it at church on Sunday. We could learn a lot from his childlike faith. Give your burdens to God today and let Him handle them. His shoulders can take that weight. ♡

Have you ever heard the old saying that we better be careful when we point our finger at someone because there are always more fingers pointing back at us? (When we point with our index finger, there are usually three other fingers folded and pointing right back at us.)

How well do you receive constructive criticism? Have you ever noticed that most of us are far better at finding the faults in others than we are at seeing the ones in ourselves?

King David had the same issue. We read about him being such a strong man of God and that even he was drawn into temptation. David took another man's wife, and this led to pregnancy, lies and murder. It was a tangled mess.

However, King David has used his power to cover most of the drama except God knew. God knows it all.

In 2 Samuel 12, God sends a man named Nathan to prick David's heart, to get his attention. Nathan uses the analogy of a wealthy man who had a fine herd of lambs and his neighbor who had one precious ewe. The wealthy man had a visitor and decided to butcher a lamb to celebrate the visit, but he didn't want to use one of his own animals, so he took the single one that his neighbor so dearly loved. Let's look at David's reaction to the story:

> "Then David's anger was greatly kindled against the man, and he said to Nathan, 'As the Lord lives, the man who has done this deserves to die'."
>
> 2 Samuel 12:5 ESV

Those are strong words from David. Nathan's reply in verse 6 is, "This man is YOU!"

The rest of this chapter (please go read 2 Samuel 12) is Nathan sharing God's anger with and disappointment in David. Does God forsake David? No. Does God turn His back on David and forget him? No. God's love is eternal, and we are His. However, this loving God is also a Father who holds us accountable and will walk with us through the consequences of our choices. ♡

●　●　●

## Pointing Fingers and Taking Correction

Question: who controls the thermostat in your house? Are there rules about the cherished thermostat? Is part of your family cold while the other part is hot? I surely am glad my husband and I have finally synced our body temps so we can agree on bumping the temperature right on down!

Consider this: What is the difference between a thermostat and a thermometer?

Have you ever considered that simple thought? One can control an area while the other is a simple reflection of the area surrounding it.

As Christians we need to set the climate and not just reflect what's around us. Our presence should be different from others; it is what sets us apart. We may not get to choose how every moment of our lives unfolds, but we DO get to choose how we react to these moments.

Are we blending into the climate and adjusting to acclimate, or are we channeling the fruits of the Spirit to impact a spiritual change in the climate?

"Go ye therefore, and teach all nations, baptizing them in the name of the Father, and of the Son, and of the Holy Ghost." Matthew 28:19 ESV

This is our charge as Christians. We are to actively share God's love in both word and action. Go be a thermostat today and positively impact the world by planting seeds of faith. ♡

Have you ever heard the old saying, "That child is the spitting image of its _____?" (I have always wondered what spit has to do with an image.) When you meet a newborn baby, do you look for its resemblance to a parent or other family members?

I think we have all admired new babies and said we could see some resemblance to someone. A Sunday School lesson had a great analogy that spoke to me.

The author of the lesson said our Christian resemblance to God evolved much like that of a newborn to its family. Babies are constantly changing their looks in those first few months and even years. Then their physical characteristics become much more settled, and we can truly see the marks of a family lineage. The same is true for our Christian lives.

We cannot expect a brand-new Christian to immediately bear a full resemblance to God; we are all in the process of growing His attributes in our own lives. However, as time goes on, we should have an increasingly marked resemblance to Christ in both word and action.

Do we resemble Christ today? Can others see Jesus in us? ♡

Sing with me... "Go tell it on the mountain, over the hills and everywhere... go tell it on the mountain that Jesus Christ is... Lord!"

I took the liberty of changing the last word; the actual lyrics say born rather than Lord. (Keep reading and you will understand why!)

Have you ever heard of the Great Commission? The definition of a commission is "an instruction, command or duty given to a person or a group of people." Now also consider that it is called THE Great Commission. Using the word *the* implies it is singularly important, like the flood (as in Noah's) or the Great Depression (as in hallelujah there has only been one).

Matthew 28 says:

> "And Jesus came and said to them, 'All authority in heaven and on earth has been given to me. Go therefore and make disciples of all nations, baptizing them in the name of the Father and of the Son and of the Holy Spirit, teaching them to observe all that I have commanded you. And behold, I am with you always, to the end of the age'."
>
> Matthew 28:18-20 ESV

This scripture is known as THE GREAT COMMISSION; it is our charge as Christians. We are to share our God with others! Now. Today. No time like the present! Go tell it on the mountain that Jesus Christ is Lord! ♡

Have you ever been told you have a poker face? I have never been a big card shark. Old Maid and Solitaire are about as deep as my interest or skill level can go, but I can definitely identify with a poker face.

I bet we have all had times when we put on a smile for the world when our insides were not feeling it. We go to work and church, hang out with friends and family and pretend all is well. Sometimes it's just not. Why do we put on the poker face?

Sometimes the struggle is just too painful to share. Sometimes we are so overwhelmed that we don't even know how to share. So we pretend.

There is never a need to pretend with God. He already knows. He is with us every moment. He hears us when we don't even know how or what to pray. He also places people in our lives at the right moments to be vessels of His love.

> "Have I not commanded you? Be strong and courageous.
> Do not be frightened, and do not be dismayed, for the Lord
> your God is with you wherever you go."
>
> Joshua 1:9 ESV

The next time you feel an urge to call a person, do it. When you run into someone at the store and have the chance to speak, do it. When you find yourself with a spare moment and a specific person pops into your brain, reach out. When you are burdened with a need to pray for a person, do it! We may not always be able to see past the poker face, but God does, and He may be allowing you the opportunity to join Him in loving a fellow person. ♡

I saw a quote that gave me pause:

"Holding onto anger is like drinking poison and expecting the other person to die."

Did you just take a deep breath? I did. Anger and hatred are justified, right? We are entitled to feel that way when wronged, correct?

Let's see what God's word says:

> "Let all bitterness and wrath and anger and clamor and slander be put away from you, along with all malice. Be kind to one another, tenderhearted, forgiving one another, as God in Christ forgave you."
>
> Ephesians 4:31-32 ESV

Geez. That is tough. Letting go of feelings of anger toward someone who has wronged us is *hard*. God knew that it would be. That is why He wove it into His word multiple times.

> Like here: "Then Peter came up and said to him, 'Lord, how often will my brother sin against me, and I forgive him? As many as seven times?' Jesus said to him, 'I do not say to you seven times, but seventy-seven times'."
>
> Matthew 18:21-22 ESV

> And here: "Bearing with one another and, if one has a complaint against another, forgiving each other; as the Lord has forgiven you, so you also must forgive."
>
> Colossians 3:13 ESV

Do we get the picture? Stop drinking the poison of anger today and pray for God to help you let it go and move on. ♡

Do you celebrate Memorial Day? Maybe you fire up the grill or enjoy some fun in the water. This is traditionally the holiday which marks the beginning of summer fun.

What is its real purpose? In 1971, the last Monday of May was officially set aside as a federal holiday to commemorate the lives of active-duty soldiers lost in combat.

Have you ever visited the Tomb of the Unknown soldier at Arlington National Cemetery in Washington, DC? This is a place that holds unidentified remains of soldiers from multiple wars. It is a sacred place that represents the sacrifice of thousands of Americans across our country's history. Every 30 minutes there is a changing of the guard. (If you ever get to see this event in person, GO!) I have stood and watched this event many times over the years, and it never loses its significance.

Here is a little-known fact: the gentlemen who serve as guards must fit the uniform; the uniform is not made to fit the guard.

Pretty specific, right? My waist might have made that cut when I was 10.

Consider this: How often do we try to make the "fit" of being a Christian match our own desires? How often do we try to justify our selfish choices to force our interpretation of Christian faith to fit our lifestyle?

God gives us clear direction in His Word on what our Christian walk should embrace. We are to be set apart; we are to be different from the world. ♡

Have you ever done something wrong and then realized it was wrong? How did you feel? What was your reaction?

I heard a great question at church last week. "What is the difference between guilt and conviction?"

Hmmm. Both mean I realize I have done something wrong. I had to ponder that for a moment. For me, the word *guilt* implies some shame and avoidance, and *conviction* implies the need to make it right. What about you?

Here was the statement that was shared: "As Christians, guilt often pulls us away from God, and conviction usually draws us closer to God."

Wow! I get that, and I have felt that. Think about Luke 22 in which Judas betrays Jesus by handing him over in exchange for money. Judas then feels guilty about what he did, and he runs away in shame. Peter also betrays Jesus in this same chapter by denying him three times. Although Peter vehemently argued that it would never happen, he did it. However, when that rooster crowed, Peter realized he had done exactly what was predicted, and Peter became convicted. He repented and got busy. He went on to become one of the strongest disciples in reaching others. He was drawn closer to God as a result of his sin.

We are born into sin. We will all make mistakes. Let's choose today to let our mistakes convict us and draw us closer in our relationships with God. He is always the answer. ♡

Do you have a morning routine? Do you have certain steps that you follow most mornings when you get up for the day? Does it get you off balance if your routine is disturbed? Maybe the alarm doesn't go off, or you forget to put on deodorant because a child was calling your name, or you have to skip breakfast because you are late.

As Christians, God calls us to have a daily routine as well.

> "Only be very careful to observe the commandment and the law that Moses the servant of the Lord commanded you, to love the Lord your God, and to walk in all His ways and to keep His commandments and to cling to Him and to serve Him with all your heart and with all your soul."
>
> Joshua 22:5 ESV

We are to love God every day, believe God every day, trust God every day and serve God every day. God doesn't want to be a piece of our lives on a couple days of the week. He wants to be the center of our lives every single day. ♡

Was there ever time in your youth that you would have preferred a spanking over "the talk"? My parents could leverage some heavy guilt. Hearing their disappointment and their counsel of why I should not have done something was a painful punishment. Several times I remember wishing they would just spank me and be done with it.

How good are we at receiving direction as adults? Do we seek and welcome wisdom, or do we wing it and hope for the best?

God speaks often on wisdom. Solomon prayed for God to give him wisdom and discernment. He went on to write the Book of Proverbs. Consider these verses:

> "Because I have called and you refused to listen, have stretched out my hand and no one has heeded, because you have ignored all my counsel and would have none of my reproof, I also will laugh at your calamity."
>
> Proverbs 1:24-26 ESV

Ouch. The idea that God would laugh at our messes seems harsh but look how often we may have turned away from His guidance. As parents, don't we sometimes have to let our children make mistakes because they think they know best?

Now consider this scripture:

> "For the Lord gives wisdom; from his mouth comes knowledge and understanding; he stores up sound wisdom for the upright; he is a shield to those who walk in integrity, guarding the paths of justice and watching over the way of His saints."
>
> Proverbs 2:6-8 ESV

We have a choice. God wants to direct us, save us from making messes. We just have to seek Him, through His word, in prayer, with fellow Christians. Let's seek to be wise in Christ today! ♡

●  ●  ●

## The Guilt Trip...the Parent Talk

Do you have a sweet tooth? I surely do. I love sugary sweets! (Almost all of them!) They draw me like birds to nectar.

While an abundance of sugar may not be good for our physical body, our spiritual and emotional needs can surely be positively affected by sweet words. Sincere, kind words can go a long way toward helping us all face the hardships of this world.

Look at this verse:

> "Gracious words are like a honeycomb, sweetness to the soul and health to the body."
>
> Proverbs 16:24 ESV

Sometimes we are far quicker to spew the negative than the positive. We need to be intentional about sharing positive thoughts with others. Rather than simply walking by and thinking how kind someone is, speak up and thank that person for the kindness. Rather than just noticing that someone always has an encouraging smile, speak up and tell that person how much you appreciate that smile each day.

Let's not take good things for granted lest they fall away. Let's commit to being kind and to recognizing kindness in others. This world is simply too hard. We need to embrace the good. ♡

Did any of you participate in the Bible Sword Drills in your youth? They were quite popular when I was a child and I excelled. Except that one time. One part of the competition required that we receive a specific verse when prompted by its "address." We were told to recite 2 Timothy 2:15. I simply could not pull it from my brain. You may think it odd that I remember that particular event. Every competitor was always given a standard black Bible to use during the competition in order to assure it was fair. After I missed this question, I looked down and realized that exact verse was partially ENGRAVED on the front of the Bible.

> "Do your best to present yourself to God as one approved,
> a worker who has no need to be ashamed, rightly handling
> the word of truth."
>
> 2 Timothy 2:15 ESV

I noticed a different part of this verse recently. My eye has always been drawn to the part about being a worker who should not be ashamed. This time, as I was reading the chapter, my eye fell to the final part: "rightly handling (dividing) the Word of Truth."

God's message here is more about His Word. As Christians, we are to study the Bible, lean on His Word and share it with others. As we share, it is very important that we share it correctly. We are not to pull single verses out of context. We are not to twist verses for our own meaning. We are not to pick and choose what parts of the Bible are ok to share and what parts to avoid. It is God's Word divinely inspired by Him. We are to read it, study it and share it! ♡

Have you seen the map pics that you can hang on the wall and "scratch off" to reveal one state at a time as you visit each? Traveling can be fun and inspirational as we get to see how differently God designed parts of our country.

Today I was reading the book of Numbers and chapter 33 gave me pause. This chapter outlines, stop by stop, the journey of Moses and the Israelites. From one verse to the next it reads, "The people of Israel set out from…". This book basically gives us a visual road map of their journey.

What about ours? Have you ever sat down and written out the stops of your journey? I don't mean this in the literal sense of travel, but rather in the spiritual sense. Where has God brought you from? What has God brought you through?

In the same sense that God commanded Moses to sit down and note the stops of their journey to remind them all where he brought them from and what he brought them through, we need to be reminded of the same.

God. Is. Faithful. He is here every step of our lives and wants to be a guide for us if we will allow Him. ♡

"What kind of church would your church be if every member was just like you?"

This question was in our lesson at church, and it gave me a whopping pause. Wow! What kind of church member am I? What kind of Christian am I? What would the church be like if there were more members like me?

It is easy for us to look at others and find faults. It is more difficult for us to look within and reflect on our own weaknesses.

> "For even the Son of Man came not to be served but to
> serve, and to give his life as a ransom for many."
> Mark 10:45 ESV

Jesus came to serve. He didn't come to "sit and get." He led by example, and we are to follow His lead. ♡

How good are you at rejoicing? Can you shout a praise, raise a hand, get excited?

Let's look in Philippians 4:

> "Rejoice in the Lord always; again, I will say, rejoice. Let your reasonableness be known to everyone. The Lord is at hand; do not be anxious about anything, but in everything by prayer and supplication with thanksgiving let your requests be made known to God. And the peace of God, which surpasses all understanding, will guard your hearts and your minds in Christ Jesus."
>
> Philippians 4:4-7 ESV

Rejoice in the Lord always. Always. I see so much heartache all around us. There are so very many people who are hurting, including me. How do we rejoice even in these times?

Because we have God who knows all and loves us. Jeremiah 29:11 says He knows the plans He has for us. God already knows the story. We must trust Him and let Him lead. (Even when it is so very hard.)

Do not be anxious about anything. Whew. I really struggle with this one. (I must not be the only one because there are millions of dollars being made each year by drug companies who sell anxiety meds). Look at that next piece. In every situation present your requests to God through prayer and petition. PRAYER and PETITION. Take it to God!

And the peace of God will guard our hearts! I am SO THANKFUL for the peace that God can give. Even amid the worst of storms, we can cling to His peace like a lifeline! ♡

Who invested in you?

Who has invested in your walk with God? Think back. Was it family? Friends? A Sunday School teacher? A pastor? A stranger?

As Christians, our eyes and hearts are to be on God and His Word. Many times, there are people on this earth who have poured into us to help direct us to God. Look at the words of Paul as he writes to Timothy:

> "I thank God whom I serve, as did my ancestors, with a clear conscience, as I remember you constantly in my prayers night and day. As I remember your tears, I long to see you, that I may be filled with joy. I am reminded of your sincere faith, a faith that dwelt first in your grandmother Lois and your mother Eunice and now, I am sure, dwells in you as well."
>
> 2 Timothy 1:3-5 ESV

Wow! Paul is still mentoring Timothy from afar, and he is encouraging him by reminding him of the faith of those who poured into him. Today I encourage you to take a moment to recall people who took the time to pray for you, nurture your faith, and direct you to God! Let's celebrate God's faithfulness in the people He sends along the way to invest in our Christian faith! ♡

I was at the beach, and I saw many things. One moment particularly gave me pause.

As I sat soaking in some warm sunshine, I watched two middle-school-aged girls work for over 30 minutes trying to get the "perfect" selfie. Both girls were so cute in their red, white and blue outfits, yet no pic seemed to work. They would take pics of each other, look at the pics, and shake their heads and begin the process again. It hurt my heart.

Why are we so consumed with appearances? Why are we so worried about how others see us? Wouldn't the world be such a better place if we could see ourselves and love ourselves the way God sees and loves us?

> "For you formed my inward parts; you knitted me together in my mother's womb. I praise you, for I am fearfully and wonderfully made. Wonderful are your works; my soul knows it very well."
>
> Psalm 139:13-14 ESV

> "For we are his workmanship, created in Christ Jesus for good works, which God prepared beforehand, that we should walk in them."
>
> Ephesians 2:10 ESV

> "Why, even the hairs of your head are all numbered. Fear not; you are of more value than many sparrows."
>
> Luke 12:7 ESV

God made us. God loves us. God chose us.

When my children were small, there were trendy onesies and t-shirts that spotted the saying, "God don't make no junk!" While the grammar may be seriously flawed, the message is amazing! God made you. God made me. We are not junk. We are just the way he wanted us to be. Let's help ourselves remember this and then pour it into our children and grandchildren. ♡

● ● ●

### Making Selfies...What Does Jesus See?

Do you have a temper? Is your temper easily provoked and quick to burn or a slow ember that takes lots of oxygen to get hot?

We all have our buttons that can set off our tempers, and these buttons can differ greatly. The real question is about how we deal with our temper when it is stirred.

The verses below step on my toes. I need to memorize them because sometimes I tend to react before thinking.

> "Have nothing to do with foolish, ignorant controversies; you know that they breed quarrels. And the Lord's servant must not be quarrelsome but kind to everyone, able to teach, patiently enduring evil, correcting others with gentleness..."
>
> 2 Timothy 2:23-24 ESV

Notice that God instructs us to be kind AND real. He doesn't expect us to simply ignore issues. He asks that we teach and correct with patience and gentleness. I wonder if that is where the old adage of "catching more flies with sugar than vinegar" was created?

When the embers of temper are stirring, hit the pause button and seek God's direction. His way may seem tough, but we can do it with His help. ♡

Have you ever encountered a stranger who already knew you? Did it startle you? Were you uncomfortable because you did not know the person? Were you worried about how this person knew you?

How will you feel when you finally meet Jesus face to face? He will know everything about you: the good, the bad, and the ugly.

Look with me in John. Phillip has met Jesus earlier in the chapter and he has run to share the good news with Nathaniel who is being a little cynical.

> "Jesus saw Nathaniel coming toward Him and said, 'Behold, an Israelite indeed, in whom there is no deceit!' Nathaniel said to Him, 'How do you know me?' Jesus answered him, 'Before Philip called you, when you were under the fig tree, I saw you'."
>
> John 1:47-48 ESV

Jesus knows us, too. What would He say to us? The day is coming when we will meet Him face to face. God knows we are sinfully imperfect. He can also see into our hearts. What will He see in us? ♡

I love a good makeover! It feels good when I give my yards a good mowing and weeding; it is exciting to see the finished product of a freshly painted and decorated room. (It isn't so fun to do the actual work of that). It is even refreshing to get a new haircut and maybe even get dressed up for a big event now and then! Makeovers can be rejuvenating!

What about a spiritual makeover? What if we truly allow God to change us? USE us?

Romans 23 gives the layout for this makeover. Look at these first two verses:

> "I appeal to you therefore, brothers, by the mercies of God, to present your bodies as a living sacrifice, holy and acceptable to God, which is your spiritual worship. Do not be conformed to this world, but be transformed by the renewal of your mind, that by testing you may discern what is the will of God, what is good and acceptable and perfect."
>
> Romans 12:1-2 ESV

God wants us to commit to Him in heart, mind and soul. Then He wants us to allow Him to mold us as vessels to share His love with others. Go read this whole chapter. It is a great guidebook for an amazing makeover! ♡

We often hear that Jesus died for our sins, right? Have you ever struggled with this truth?

You may wonder which sins? How many sins? You may think your sins make you unworthy; that is simply not true.

Look at this scripture:

Psalm 103:
"As far as the east is from the west,
so far does he remove our transgressions from us."

Did you see that? Jesus removes all of our sin when we accept Him into our lives. Jesus knew on that cross that you and I were not even born yet and that we would be imperfect humans; He knew we would sin. He chose to die for us. We just have to accept this gift into our hearts and allow Him to lead us.

Look at this scripture:

Psalm 32:
"1 Blessed is the one whose transgression is forgiven,
whose sin is covered.
2 Blessed is the man against whom the Lord counts no iniquity,
and in whose spirit there is no deceit.

5 I acknowledged my sin to you,
and I did not cover my iniquity;
I said, 'I will confess my transgressions to the Lord,'
and you forgave the iniquity of my sin."

Jesus forgives, and Jesus loves. Just ask. Have a talk with Him in prayer. It doesn't have to be fancy words because it is just a conversation with the best listener you will ever meet. He already knows; He is simply waiting for us to ask. ♡

July 2: Did you know this is the date that the Declaration of Independence was actually said to have been signed? Yes, we celebrate the 4th of July because that is the date it was officially made public. However, the meeting of the signing was two days earlier. So why keep it quiet?

These 56 men were inviting havoc into their lives by signing their names. This document was being sent to the king, their *ruler*. It was going to bring the mighty British army across the ocean to get the colonies under control; it would be the beginning of a war.

Two things stand out to me: 1) These men knew the American colonies were the underdogs, and they knew that the coming battle would not be easy and there were no guarantees of success; 2) They took a stand of great personal sacrifice by letting their signatures place targets directly on them. (5 were tortured and killed, 12 lost their homes, 9 fought and died from injuries, and the list goes on).

Consider this scripture from Ephesians 6:

> "In all circumstances take up the shield of faith, with which you can extinguish all the flaming darts of the evil one; and take the helmet of salvation, and the sword of the Spirit, which is the word of God."
>
> Ephesians 6:16-17 ESV

Don't you wonder if these same words gave these folks courage all of those years ago? There are multiple sources of evidence that these Founding Fathers of our nation were rooted in Christian faith. Were they perfect? No. Did they make mistakes? Yes. Did God impact their lives and the future of our country? Indeed.

Freedoms we have, especially the freedom to worship God. Just as God was with these people generations ago, He is with us today. He doesn't promise that life will always be easy, but He does promise to be right beside us for each step as we seek to glorify Him. ♡

• • •

## Are We Willing to Sign on the Dotted Line?

Have you seen a beautiful sunset? I have seen pics all over social media of the glorious masterpieces that God paints across the sky. No filters needed.

Do you understand that we are His masterpieces, too? He sees beauty in us that we cannot sometimes see in ourselves. He made us; He designed us. We are each one of His creations.

> "For we are his masterpiece, created in Christ Jesus for good works, which God prepared beforehand, that we should walk in them."
>
> Ephesians 2:10 ESV

> "For you formed my inward parts; you knitted me together in my mother's womb. I praise you, for I am fearfully and wonderfully made. Wonderful are your works; my soul knows it very well."
>
> Psalm 139:13-14 ESV

Next time you see that beautiful sunset or sunrise, when you see God's creation in splendid form, pause and remember that you are His creation, too. You are His masterpiece as well, and He loves you beyond measure! ♡

"The hip bone's connected to the back bone. The back bone's connected to the neck bone. The neck bone's connected to the head bone." Do you remember this children's song from years ago? It goes through the connections of many bones in the body with such a catchy tune!

Have you ever thought about your purpose? A note I had jotted in the back of my Bible caught my eye today. It says, "Change me, use me" and has Romans 12 noted next to it. I decided to go refresh my memory. Look at these scriptures.

> "For as in one body we have many members, and the members do not all have the same function, so we, though many, are one body in Christ, and individually members one of another. Having gifts that differ according to the grace given to us, let us use them: if prophecy, in proportion to our faith; if service, in our serving; the one who teaches, in his teaching; the one who exhorts, in his exhortation; the one who contributes, in generosity; the one who leads, with zeal; the one who does acts of mercy, with cheerfulness."
>
> Romans 12:4-8 ESV

The early part of this chapter (go read the whole chapter because it's good stuff!) tells us to give our bodies to God and not to conform to the world. We are to be living and holy sacrifices (v 1-2). The scripture above commands us to use the talents God has given us. Just like the bones in the body, we as Christians have different talents; however, we can unite these talents into one mighty purpose: to form a body of believers who serve our King!

I encourage you to ponder this phrase today, "Change me, use me, Lord!" ♡

When was the last time you went to the doctor? Most of us don't relish those visits or those bills.

Jesus used an analogy of going to the doctor in the book of Matthew. Jesus had just called Matthew to be a disciple and they were "hanging out" with some other tax collectors (those folks were considered unsavory) and some "other" sinners (we don't know what exactly these folks were known for). The Pharisees (the local religion police) were turning their noses up at Jesus for associating with these lowly folks. Here is Jesus's response:

> "But when he heard it, he said, 'Those who are well have no need of a physician, but those who are sick. Go and learn what this means: 'I desire mercy, and not sacrifice.' For I came not to call the righteous, but sinners'."
>
> Matthew 9:12-13 ESV

Jesus taught a great lesson here. As Christians, we are called to share His love with others. We cannot sit around together and look down on others; we are to go out and BE THE LOVE of Christ. We are not to sit in a seat of judgment. That is for God. We are to point others to Christ.

We must remember that we are ALL sinners. None of us are perfect. Consider this verse from the book of Luke:

> "Therefore I tell you, her sins, which are many, are forgiven—for she loved much. But he who is forgiven little, loves little."
>
> Luke 7:47 ESV

We must humble ourselves daily and ask for forgiveness of our own sins (and yes, we all have them). Then we are called to connect with other sinners and point them to Christ. ♡

"There's doing what is easy and there is doing what is right."

I read this nugget of wisdom. Wouldn't it be so nice if right and easy were always paired together? It is easy and right to love my babies. It is easy and right to enjoy God's creation on a beautiful spring day.

What about other things? What about avoiding temptations? Avoiding sin? What about going against your friends in order to go with God? What about giving our tithes to God? What about being honest even when it is uncomfortable? What about spending meaningful time with God?

These things should be easy, but sometimes they aren't.
God is clear about doing the right thing in His eyes:

> "So whoever knows the right thing to do and fails to do it,
> for him it is sin."
>
> James 4:17 ESV

God is also He who sees and blesses us for doing what is right. There are many times in my life when I have done the wrong thing (even when my gut was screaming *no!*), and I have paid the consequences. In addition, there are many times I have done the right thing, even when it is tough, and God has blessed me beyond measure.

> "But even if you should suffer for righteousness' sake, you
> will be blessed. Have no fear of them, nor be troubled."
>
> 1 Peter 3:14 ESV

I am thankful that we serve a God who not only loves but also grows us. A Father who directs us in His path, even when the directing may require nudges to get us back on track. ♡

Are you a doubter? Maybe even a skeptic? Do the events of Easter seem too hard to believe? Do you sometimes have trouble understanding or accepting?

It is ok to not understand. It is ok to be a little unsure. Even the disciples didn't fully understand.

> "Both of them were running together, but the other disciple outran Peter and reached the tomb first. And stooping to look in, he saw the linen cloths lying there, but he did not go in. Then Simon Peter came, following him, and went into the tomb. He saw the linen cloths lying there, and the face cloth, which had been on Jesus' head, not lying with the linen cloths but folded up in a place by itself. Then the other disciple, who had reached the tomb first, also went in, and he saw and believed; for as yet they did not understand the Scripture, that he must rise from the dead."
>
> John 20:4-9 ESV

Notice they ran and then stopped. The "other" disciple didn't even go in until Peter went in first.

Pay particular attention to the last part of verse 9. These guys have been with Jesus for years and they STILL don't get it. They WILL get it, but they don't yet.

If you sometimes struggle with fully understanding the Bible, relax. We all do. If you sometimes struggle with understanding what God is doing in your life, relax. We all do.

Keep seeking Him through prayer and scripture; He will fit the pieces together perfectly in His time. ♡

Can you remember your Mama's stern voice from childhood? Think back for a minute and pull that tone into focus in your mind. Got it? Now, did you ever hear her say, "BE STILL!!!" I have no problem hearing my Mama saying those words many times in my childhood, especially during church.

Did you know our Father God says the same thing? Read with me.

> "Be still, and know that I am God: I will be exalted among the nations, I will be exalted in the earth!"
>
> Psalm 46:10 ESV

Be still. Be still, and know that I am God. KNOW THAT I AM GOD! Does that excite you? It should. God is GOD! He knows our worries. He knows our challenges. He knows our sins. He LOVES us. He MADE us!

Be encouraged today and rest in His arms. Just be still during all that may be going on around you and know that God is right there with you. ♡

*Trust.* Small word but a big action.

> "Trust in the Lord with all your heart and lean not on your own understanding. In all your ways acknowledge Him and He will direct your path."
>
> Proverbs 3:5-6 ESV

I memorized these verses as a child, probably during Bible Sword Drill days. You could utter the first three words and my mind would immediately complete the scripture. I know it. I understand it.

I sometimes struggle with embracing it fully. The world teaches us to lean on our own understanding, to take the bull by the horns and act. God says to trust Him, let Him lead.

This makes me think of a quote by Dr. Martin Luther King, Jr. "Faith is taking the first step when you cannot see the rest of the staircase."

If you need encouragement today, breathe these verses into your heart and your life. He will truly direct our paths, especially when we cannot see the way. ♡

As a child, I thought that the Declaration of Independence came AFTER the American Revolution once we had defeated Britain. This document was the firestarter of the revolution. The colonies reached their tipping point of the control of King George. Since he was located an ocean away, the colonists drafted a written document to let him know not only that they were done, but also WHY they were done. This famous document went through 86 drafts before a final draft was ready. Wow. 86 changes before they reached the full message.

Isn't this somewhat like our Christian lives? While accepting Christ into our hearts is a life-changing event, it is not the end. Becoming a Christian does not mean we go from sinful to sinless. We will seek to become more and more like Christ, and there will be times we will fail. There will be many "drafts" as we grow and learn to truly walk in faith.

Thomas Jefferson was not able to attend the 50th celebration of the Declaration of Independence, but he wrote these words about it:

"May it be to the world, what I believe it will be, the signal of arousing men to burst free of their chains…"

Whew! Take that visual image to our Christian walk. Accepting salvation IS all about breaking chains! It is about being set free from the chains of the world and living freely in the promises of God.

As we celebrate our nation's independence (any day of the year), let's remember that our blessings come from God, both as a nation and as individuals. Let's love each other and remember that our Christian walks become stronger as we go through our "drafts" of learning and growing to walk for Jesus. ♡

Is there an empty parking place at the church? When was the last time you saw the church parking lot full for a worship service? (We aren't counting weddings and funerals and such.)

I remember a time when I saw ours full; I had to park on the side of the highway and walk past tons of vehicles to get to the front door. It was on a Tuesday evening, September 2001. It was over twenty years ago on September 11, on the day terrorists rocked our world.

We had an impromptu prayer service that evening, and it was amazing. People came. People fell on their knees. People prayed. What is that scripture?

> "If people who are called by my name humble themselves, and pray and seek my face and turn from their wicked ways, then I will hear from heaven and will forgive their sin and heal their land."
>
> 2 Chronicles 7:14 ESV

Yes. That scripture.

We have empty parking places today. What about you? We have some empty pews, too. Why do we have to be so stubborn? Why does it take tragedy and fear to get us on our knees?

The even sadder part? God doesn't need us; He wants us.

> "He answered, "I tell you, if these were silent, the very stones would cry out'."
>
> Luke 19:40 ESV

I don't want rocks to have to sound out praise to Jesus as long as I am drawing breath. Jesus wants our praise in both the good and the bad times. He wants us to choose to walk with Him.

Let's do our part. Invite folks to church. Be the Christian that inspires people through our words and actions to want to come to church. ♡

● ● ●

## Are there empty parking places at your church?

Have you ever failed? Maybe you started a Pinterest project and discovered it was not as simple as it looked. Maybe you tried a new recipe, and it became a treat for the pets.

Maybe you have experienced a more serious failure like losing a job or causing an accident or letting someone down; those kinds of mistakes can really weigh us down.

Lucky for us that we know Jesus. He can redeem our failures and use them to grow us into better people. Failure can be a great teacher if we will embrace the humility that is required for us to be able to learn.

Consider Peter. He appeared to be one of the strongest disciples for Jesus, and then he failed. He denied Jesus three times in one night in Luke 22. He was ashamed, but Jesus. Isn't that a great phrase? "But Jesus..." Jesus intervened and helped grow Peter into an even stronger advocate for salvation. Jesus will do the same for us if we allow Him.

I worry sometimes in today's "everybody gets a trophy" world. There is a perception that failure isn't an option. I disagree. Failure is a reality that we will all experience from time to time. We are imperfect humans; we make mistakes. The question is how will we react to these life lessons? Will we humble ourselves and seek God and grow? That decision is up to us. I choose Jesus. What about you? ♡

There was a sit-com called *I Love Lucy* that featured the hilarity of Lucille Ball and her comrades. I bet you have seen at least some snippets of episodes.

Do you remember the grape-crushing scene? The one where Lucy must climb into the vat of grapes and stomp them with her bare feet? I saw it as a child and have always thought it would be pretty cool to do (after gagging over the fact that bare feet were impacting something that would be processed to drink).

Think about the crushing of the grapes. The crushing yields a wonderful product of grape juice. The pressing of olives releases a wonderful oil that we use in cooking. A sparkling diamond is formed from the pressure of the immense weight of rock. (Are you seeing a trend?)

Sometimes the most amazing things come from the most intense pressures. Could a struggle you are enduring today produce a blessing for tomorrow? Are you allowing God to use the season you are in to deepen your faith? Whether big or small, God loves for us to bring our problems to Him. He wants to walk with us through our storms and even carry us when the burdens become too heavy to bear. ♡

# Old Fashioned Tea Cakes

1 cup shortening
2 cups sugar
3 eggs
1 tbsp vanilla
2 cups all-purpose flour
1 cup self-rising flour
½ cup cane syrup

Cream the shortening and sugar together. Add the eggs and mix well. Add both types of flour slowly and mix well. Add the vanilla and the cane syrup. Preheat the oven to 350° and grease a cookie sheet or line it with parchment paper. Dump spoons of dough onto the sheet at least 3 inches apart. Bake for 8-10 minutes. Remove and let sit before removing from the cookie sheet.

● ● ●

Somewhere in the foggy recesses of my childhood mind, I remember eating these cookies. They were AMAZING! However, I have no idea who made them. I suspect it was my Granny Bonnie or someone from her side of the family. I am certain that my Papa Dorris's cane syrup was used to make this heavenly treat. I have had to tinker with this recipe over the years until I finally recreated what my mind remembered.

I have such fond memories of the cane-grindings that happened every fall at their home. Scan the code to come join my son and me as he learns how to make one of his favorite treats!

## Old Fashioned Tea Cakes

Did anything feel surreal during the pandemic? Almost like it wasn't real. It may be the first time in our lives that we can personally identify with the confusion that folks might have felt the day after Jesus—the healer, the teacher, the fisher of men, the miracle worker—died.

He died. They didn't expect that just like we didn't expect to be sheltered at home, just like we cannot believe schools are out, sports are canceled, and businesses are failing, all in the blink of an eye.

Imagine that "day after" all those years ago. Just that Sunday they had been cheering as Jesus rode into town on a donkey, and they laid palm fronds on his path. How could he be dead? How could the person who talked of Heaven and God and salvation and eternity be *dead*?

We know the rest of this story because we know Sunday is coming, and our Christ will rise from that grave!!!!! But for the people living in the midst of it, they couldn't understand. The disciples were frightened and scattered, and Peter had even denied Jesus. Mary and others were mourning. This was not what they had expected.

There are times when life is not what we expected either, but here is what we can do: WE CAN WORSHIP! We can seek our quiet place and lift our eyes to Heaven and praise the Lord that Jesus came for us, that He died for us. If you are feeling a little lost in the sudden shift of normal life right now, know that God is in our midst. He has a plan just like He had the perfect plan all those years ago. That tomb was empty because Jesus defeated the grave! Have hope today, and don't let fear of the unknown rule your heart. Our God has got this! ♡

Have you ever read the history of the Labor Day holiday? In the late 1800s our nation was experiencing the Industrial Revolution as many people moved from working in agriculture to working in industry. As this number grew, a controversy arose due to the low pay for extraordinarily long hours and the terribly unsafe work conditions for many. These arguments led to protests and the creation of labor unions. On September 5, 1882, over 10,000 NYC industrial workers took unpaid leave creating a march to prove a point: they had collective power, and working conditions had to change. It wasn't until 12 years later that President Cleveland signed to make Labor Day an official holiday. It now marks the official end of summer and usually includes parties, cookouts, and parades in various parts of the nation.

Thinking of this story brings a hymn to mind: "We'll work 'til Jesus Comes." I am super thankful to have better working conditions than those in the 1800s. I am more concerned today about the working hearts of us as Christians. I worry that we are becoming lackadaisical. Are we truly working to spread the love of God? Are we actively seeking to share the salvation plan with others? Are we striving to be the hands and feet of Jesus and allowing Him to use us as vessels for Him?

As you enjoy the next Labor Day holiday, please pause and consider your work for Jesus. Where could you grow? I know I have room to improve, and I bet that is true for almost everyone. ♡

What moves you? What spurs you into action? Is it a tied sporting event? Is it a loud concert? Is it a new baby being born? Is it the smell of your favorite food cooking? What gets you excited?

Now ask yourself: Do you get that excited about God? Are we spurred into action for Him? Does our worship match or exceed our excitement for other things?

> "Praise the Lord! Praise the Lord, O my soul! I will praise the Lord as long as I live; I will sing praises to my God while I have my being."
>
> Psalm 146:1-2 ESV

While we have our being, while we are on earth, are we praising Him? Are we excited? Do we make others wonder what we are so excited about? Is our excitement for God contagious? ♡

Have you ever felt like life is simply coming too fast? Maybe you have too many responsibilities on your plate or maybe you have major decisions to make and not enough time to consider them. Maybe you are simply in a life season in which it is just a lot.

Isn't it great to know our God can handle it? Isn't it amazing to know that He will walk right beside us and even carry us when it is necessary? Take heart in this scripture:

> "Come to me, all who labor and are heavy laden, and I will give you rest. Take my yoke upon you, and learn from me, for I am gentle and lowly in heart, and you will find rest for your souls. For my yoke is easy, and my burden is light."
> Matthew 11:28-30 ESV

Let's bind ourselves to Jesus and let Him lead the way. He already knows the path. ♡

Have you ever drawn your name in the dirt? Maybe you left someone a sweet message in the sand on the beach? One of my favorite scriptures in the Bible is about Jesus drawing in the dirt.

Read with me in John 8:

> "The scribes and the Pharisees brought a woman who had been caught in adultery and placing her in the midst they said to him, "Teacher, this woman has been caught in the act of adultery. Now in the Law, Moses commanded us to stone such women. So what do you say?" This they said to test him, that they might have some charge to bring against him. Jesus bent down and wrote with his finger on the ground. And as they continued to ask him, he stood up and said to them, 'Let him who is without sin among you be the first to throw a stone at her.' And once more he bent down and wrote on the ground. But when they heard it, they went away one by one, beginning with the older ones, and Jesus was left alone with the woman standing before him. Jesus stood up and said to her, 'Woman, where are they? Has no one condemned you? 'She said, 'No one, Lord. And Jesus said, 'Neither do I condemn you; go, and from now on sin no more'."
>
> John 8:3-11 ESV

Do you see how cool this is? These leaders of the area are trying to prove a point with Jesus, but our amazing Savior turned the point right back to them. They are publicly accusing this woman and using the law of the Old Testament against her. They want to see how Jesus will react. Do you see what he did? Jesus drew in the sand!!!!

We don't get a full explanation of what he drew, but it must have been powerful because the accusers left, one by one. It seems that Jesus quietly and calmly drew out their own sins in the sand and then told them that any of them without sin could cast the first stone. He KNEW their sins. He showed them that He knew their sins by listing them in the sand. They walked away.

Do you understand that we are ALL sinners? None of us are perfect. And do you know that Jesus still loves us? Look at what He said to the woman. He didn't ignore that she had sinned. He corrected her and instructed her not to continue in her sin, but He did NOT condemn her.

Jesus loves us and wants to grow us and teach us. Jesus wants us to love each other even when we don't agree and point each other toward Him. ♡

●　●　●

## Drawing in the Sand...Jesus knew.

Do you like roses? What is it that makes these flowers so popular? Is it the fragrance? The colors? The symbol of love?

I have often heard Jesus referred to as the Rose of Sharon, and I decided to do a little reading. It seems that Sharon was an actual location (not the name of a woman) in the Bible. It was known for being a fertile plain which produced some of the most beautiful plants and flowers. It also seems that the rose was a very desirable and precious flower even in Biblical times. Therefore, referencing Jesus as the "rose of Sharon" means He is the very best of the best. He is held above all others. (I get it!)

So this reading led me to thinking: what fragrance do I give off? What flower am I associated with? In my Christian walk, do I live a daily life that is "fragrant and appealing" with God's love? Or am I a stinkweed that pushes others away? I bet, if we are all truthful, we have all been some of both.

God calls us to love.

> "So now faith, hope, and love abide, these three; but the greatest of these is love."
>
> 1 Corinthians 13:13 ESV

Faith, hope and love. And the *greatest* of these is love. I encourage us all to check our "fragrance" today and live like we want to join Jesus in Sharon. ♡

I saw a rainbow in the sky yesterday. What is the first word that comes to your mind when you see one? For me, it is the word *promises*.

> "And God said, 'This is the sign of the covenant that I make between me and you and every living creature that is with you, for all future generations: I have set my bow in the cloud, and it shall be a sign of the covenant between me and the earth'."
>
> Genesis 9:12-13 ESV

God made a promise that He would never destroy the earth again by flood. He has kept His word.

There are numerous promises in the Bible. God promised to send a Savior. Promise kept. God promised to be with us always. Promise kept. God promised that if we confess and admit we are sinners, he will forgive our sins. Promise kept.

How good are we at making promises? What is our word worth? Do we mean what we say? I am so thankful for a Heavenly Father who does not sway; He is the same yesterday, today, tomorrow and forever (Hebrews 13:8). ♡

Do you prepare for hurricane season? Do you buy batteries and bottled water and make sure you have extra necessities in case the electricity goes out for several days? Do you listen to the warnings to prepare?

I have been reading articles about the collapse of some condos recently. It is heartbreaking. Over 100 people are still missing and are presumed dead. Do you know what is even more saddening? There are numerous accounts of warnings that were issued to the building owners and even a possible letter to the residents. Why didn't the warnings work? Maybe busy life got in the way. Maybe folks were too busy to ask more questions. Maybe they thought it would never amount to anything major. Maybe it was too costly to try to move somewhere else. there are always the "what ifs."

What if Jesus came today?

Yep. What if Jesus came today? Are we ready? Have we listened to the lessons? Have we heeded the warnings? Have we fought the good fight? Have we lived a faith that has produced fruit?

The Bible promises that Jesus will return. Are we ready? Choose to live each day as if this is THE DAY. ♡

Have you ever licked an envelope to seal it? Yes, me, too! I was very thankful when some genius invented those peel and stick stamps.

I am a bit of a history nerd and like to share tidbits of info. Did you know that kings wore signet rings unique to them? When they wanted to send a secure written message, the paper would be folded, and a drop of hot wax was placed on the fold and the king pressed his ring into the wax to give it the official seal of the king. Pretty cool, huh?

Did you know that Christians have been sealed by the one and only King of all Kings? Look at this scripture in Ephesians 1:

> "In him you also, when you heard the word of truth, the gospel of your salvation, and believed in him, were sealed with the promised Holy Spirit, who is the guarantee of our inheritance until we acquire possession of it, to the praise of his glory."
>
> Ephesians 1:13-14 ESV

We are sealed with the promise of the Holy Spirit who lives in our hearts. It is the Holy Spirit who nudges us to act for God and who gives us the gut feelings to avoid unwise decisions.

Here is a question for us to consider: Are our lives displaying the King's official seal as a child of God? ♡

Do you like to be right? Are you guilty of saying (or thinking), "I've got this!" Guilty.

I have heard the saying "a bull in a china shop" meaning someone just barrels through wreaking havoc along the way. Again, guilty. Most of us are probably guilty of acting without thinking things through, without seeking wisdom, without seeking God.

Look at this verse:

> "Every way of a man is right in his own eyes, but the Lord weighs the heart."
>
> Proverbs 21:2 ESV

We are blessed with great minds, minds that can come up with ways to make sense of our reasoning, to make excuses for our mistakes, to justify our actions (maybe these minds aren't such a blessing, huh?). We can try to prove that we knew best, BUT God knows our hearts. God knows our "why." He knows if our motivation is selfish or envious or vengeful. He knows when we are sincere and truthful and gracious. God knows us.

God gave us minds to think, to give us the option to CHOOSE Him. He wants us to seek Him and hear Him. He wants us to love Him and follow Him. ♡

Have you ever looked at someone else's life and had a little envy? I don't mean the green monster of jealousy, but just a wistfulness of wishing. The thought goes more like, "Oh! That is so sweet or great! I wish…"

I had a thought like that recently. I saw a precious family on FB enjoying what appeared to be a wonderful vacation together. My first thought was how happy they all looked. My next thought was wishing for the days when I could still round up all my bunch at the same time for a family vacation (That seems to become very difficult as they become adults).

Back to that family. Within days of that pic, a doctor's visit resulted in a life-altering diagnosis. In the blink of an eye, life changed. It was both unexpected and unwanted.

Look at this scripture from James 4:

> "Yet you do not know what tomorrow will bring. What is your life? For you are a mist that appears for a little time and then vanishes."
>
> James 4:14 ESV

Life really is a vapor. None of us know what the future holds. Life is also a gift, a wonderful, amazing opportunity. Is it easy? No. Is it perfect? Nope. Is it a treasure? Yes! What are we doing with this life? Are we showing God how thankful we are for this life by using it for His glory? Are we thanking Him daily for the blessing of life, even when it may feel bumpy and incomplete? Let's make the most of today and tomorrow and every day God allows us. ♡

I wish_____ (fill in the blank). What do you wish for? What part of your life do you wish you could improve? Do you wish you could have better overall health? Do you wish envy didn't creep in about what others have? Do you wish you were more optimistic? Do you wish you could be a better parent or spouse?

Consider this thought: Your desire to change must be greater than your desire to stay the same.

Wow! So simple, yet so true. Look at this scripture:

> "I appeal to you therefore, brothers, by the mercies of God, to present your bodies as a living sacrifice, holy and acceptable to God, which is your spiritual worship. Do not be conformed to this world, but be transformed by the renewal of your mind, that by testing you may discern what is the will of God, what is good and acceptable and perfect."
> Romans 12:1-2 ESV

Our desire to truly change must be greater than our temptation to stay in the rut of routine that we are in. Why aren't we seeing the positive changes in our lives that we desire? Could it be because we aren't putting feet on those prayers by actually pursuing our goals with fervor and commitment? Transformation is within our reach if we are willing to let go and let God. ♡

Have you ever made a recipe that was supposed to taste amazing, and it didn't?

I have had cakes flop because I used the wrong kind of flour or forgot to include the eggs. I once made cookies that tasted like salt because I misread the recipe. Regardless, I have learned that the ingredients I put into food greatly affect the taste I receive from the food.

Isn't love much the same way? What we put into love often is reflected in what we get back.

We are to love like Christ loves us.

> "When he had washed their feet and put on his outer garments and resumed his place, he said to them, 'Do you understand what I have done to you? You call me Teacher and Lord, and you are right, for so I am. If I then, your Lord and Teacher, have washed your feet, you also ought to wash one another's feet'."
>
> John 13:12-14 ESV

> "And walk in love, as Christ loved us and gave himself up for us..."
>
> Ephesians 5:2 ESV

Relationships are hard. They take work. They take sacrifice. They take love. The best ones bloom from the love of Christ because that kind of love is impossible on our own. ♡

Hustle, bustle. Hustle bustle. I love the holidays because of the time with family and friends, the good food, the laughter and the smiles. There can be so many great things going on that life becomes super busy. We aren't the first folks to have busy lives. Look at these folks all the way back in the Old Testament:

> "Thus says the Lord of hosts: These people say the time has not yet come to rebuild the house of the Lord." Then the word of the Lord came by the hand of Haggai the prophet, "Is it a time for you yourselves to dwell in your paneled houses, while this house lies in ruins? Now, therefore, thus says the Lord of hosts: Consider your ways. You have sown much and harvested little. You eat, but you never have enough; you drink, but you never have your fill. You clothe yourselves, but no one is warm. And he who earns wages does so to put them into a bag with holes."
>
> Haggai 1:2-6 ESV

Let me give you the South Georgia translation: God said, "Do you mean to tell me that you have my house in shambles while you are putting decorated trees in your house and Santa's on your lawn? You have time to watch Thanksgiving Day football games and money to buy presents to go under the tree, but no time to serve Me or money to grow My church? Is that what you mean?"

Ouch! Toes stomped. As we enter this season of Thanksgiving and Christmas, let's remember our priorities. Jesus is the reason for EVERY day, not just this season. Don't create a need for God to send us a Haggai to deliver an eye-opener. ♡

Consider this statement:

"We have to pray with our eyes on God, not on the difficulties."

Have the difficulties in your life ever consumed your focus? Do they seem to become bigger and bigger in your lens of life? Many times this can be true for most of us. However, God wants our focus to be on Him.

Consider in John 13 when Jesus is having the Last Supper with His disciples and He knows what He is about to face in the coming days. He knows how difficult His life is about to become for you and me, for our sins.

We also know that Jesus struggled some with this plan based on his prayers later that night while in the garden praying. Look at this verse during the supper:

> "Jesus knew that the Father had given all things into his
> hands, and that he had come from God and was going back
> to God."
>
> John 13:3 ESV

Even during what would be His worst difficulty during His time as a human on Earth, Jesus knew that He was in God's hands and His focus was on God. One day, as Christians, we will all return to God in Heaven. We must remember this as we journey through the trials of life. Be encouraged and know that God is with us. ♡

Have you ever made bad choices in romance? (I bet you just cringed, right? Thought of those past choices that may not have been the wisest?)

I was reading the story of Samson and Delilah this week and was struck by his failure to respond to the obvious. (You can read the whole story in Judges 16.)

The scripture notes that Sampson loved Delilah (verse 4). However, it is never noted that she felt the same. How often are we like Samson? We have strong feelings for someone (romantically or friendly) and we ignore the clear signs that feelings are not mutual.

Samson was blessed with excessive strength by God. It seemed to be strength equal to that we see in movies with superheroes. His enemies wanted him to lose that strength and hired Delilah to use her wiles to discover the secret to his strength.

> "So Delilah said to Samson, 'Please tell me where your great strength lies, and how you might be bound, that one could subdue you'."
>
> Judges 16:6 ESV

While there will always be evil folks in this world who dislike others, as Christians, we need to heed God's warnings when He seeks to protect us from unhealthy relationships. Delilah tried to trick Samson, one, two, three, FOUR times into telling the secret to his strength.

> "And she said to him, 'How can you say, 'I love you,' when your heart is not with me? You have mocked me these three times, and you have not told me where your great strength lies'."
>
> Judges 16:15 ESV

On the fourth time, she threw in the guilt of his love, and he told her the truth. She immediately had his head shaved causing the loss of Samson's strength.

Why would Samson have thought this could end any differently? She had repeatedly shown her true colors. Aren't we sometimes the same? Don't we often enter friendships or romances when the warning signs are clearly there? Do we just wear blinders? Do we think we will love them into changing?

Are there signs you are ignoring today? Is God trying to direct your path and you aren't seeing it? Seek Him. His path is always right. ♡

● ● ●

## Bad Choices in Romance?

Do you like to window shop? (Or in the day of technology, screen shop?) You know, walk through the store or scroll through an app on your phone and just browse? I do. I like to see the new trends, the bargains, etc. I have been known to ride through car dealerships just to see what bells and whistles the newer models offer or drive through subdivisions to see the new homes that have been built.

No harm, right? Right. Unless, unless these actions are creating a desire to constantly get what we do not have. Unless we are seeking fulfillment through possessions rather than through Christ. Look at this verse:

> "And he said to them, 'Take care, and be on your guard against all covetousness, for one's life does not consist in the abundance of his possessions'."
>
> Luke 12:15 ESV

Jesus goes on in this chapter to caution against greed. He cautions us to be thankful for our blessings and to use them for God's glory rather than always storing them up for ourselves.

Don't get me wrong; we buy new stuff. We update things. However, God asks us to search for our motivations. Why are we doing this? He cautions us not to let possessions become our idols. In these times of technology, the ability to browse is greater than ever, and the temptations to constantly upgrade can be overwhelming. Remember that all our blessings come from God, and He is the source of our fulfillment. (And there is no newer and better model of Him!) ♡

Imagine that it is the day after Thanksgiving. Be honest; are you on a carb overload? I am. Whew! Those traditional comfort foods like turkey and dressing and casseroles are amazing!

Have you ever read about how the Thanksgiving holiday came to be established? I don't mean the first Thanksgiving that is often referenced in grade school as students reenact the sharing of a meal between the Pilgrims and the Native Americans. I am speaking of the official declaration of the last Thursday in November being set aside as Thanksgiving Day in the United States.

The year was 1863, and the Civil War was more heated than either side had expected and what was thought would be one skirmish had now become a war that was barreling through multiple years with no end in sight. President Abraham Lincoln shared these words on October 3, 1863, as he signed to create this national holiday:

"No human counsel hath devised nor hath any mortal hand worked out these great things. They are the gracious gifts of the Most High God, who, while dealing with us in anger for our sins, hath nevertheless remembered mercy. It has seemed to me fit and proper that they should be solemnly, reverently and gratefully acknowledged as with one heart and one voice by the whole American people."

Even amid great turmoil, Lincoln could see blessings from God. As the leader of the United States, he felt that the nation should pause to give thanks to God. There is a good lesson there. We all need to give thanks every day for the mercy He has shown us, and we need to allow God to be the central focus of our lives. ♡

Do you look for certain landmarks as you drive? Do you like someone to give you directional landmarks? For example, "Turn at the second road on the left and just past the first curve, look for the big oak tree on the right and you should see our driveway with a red mailbox."

I like landmarks. It is amazing to me how decades may pass, and I can revisit a landmark of my youth and immediately release a flood of memories associated with that place.

Have you ever heard of the name Ebenezer? (You're probably envisioning a scene from the Christmas movie, right?) I am speaking of a different Ebenezer. Look with me in the Bible:

> "Then Samuel took a stone and set it up between Mizpah and Shen and called its name Ebenezer, saying, 'Thus far the Lord has helped us'."
>
> 1 Samuel 7:12 ESV

The Israelites had been under attack both from inside and out. Some of the people within their camp had begun worshiping idols. Then they came under attack by the Philistines. God used Samuel to redirect them, and they turned their focus back to God. God then turned the Philistines away through His mighty presence. (Go read all of chapter 7.)

After everything settled down, Samuel placed a stone marker and called it Ebenezer to remind them that God helped them at this very place.

Look at your life: where are your "Ebenezers"? Where has God been your source of mighty help? Do you need to revisit some of these mental landmarks to remind you today of how much God loves you and that He is with you all the time, even in the midst of life's most difficult spots? ♡

# Granny Wylena's Icebox Fruitcake

1 can condensed milk
1 16-ounce bag miniature marshmallows
2 packs graham cracker crumbs
½-1 cup pecans
1 cup chopped candied cherries

Combine condensed milk and marshmallows on low heat in a saucepan. Stir until melted together. Stir in pecans and cherries. (Use more or less nuts as you prefer; I'm not as big a fan as my hubby.) Add the graham cracker crumbs slowly and stir. (You may not need all the crumbs if you use more nuts.)

Dump mixture onto parchment paper. Separate into four equal mounds. Roll each into a roll that is about 2 inches in diameter. Wrap in parchment paper and set in the refrigerator or freezer in an airtight container. The cakes will keep for two months. Remove and thaw and slice into ½ inch cookies.

● ● ●

This is a recipe that has been in my Christmas memories forever. My Granny always had them made in advance for any family or church gathering. They also make GREAT gifts! Scan the code to join my cousins and me as we make this recipe and reminisce about Friday nights at Granny's house!

## Granny's Icebox Fruitcake

SCAN ME

Were any of your babies bald as toddlers? Did you wait eagerly for them to grow some hair? God gave me some lessons in patience with all of my babies when it came to hair growth.

Did you know God knows the number of hairs on your head? Seriously. He said it in the Bible.

> "Are not five sparrows sold for two pennies? And not one of them is forgotten before God. Why, even the hairs of your head are all numbered. Fear not; you are of more value than many sparrows."
>
> Luke 12:6-7 ESV

> "Are not two sparrows sold for a penny? And not one of them will fall to the ground apart from your Father. But even the hairs of your head are all numbered."
>
> Matthew 10:29-30 ESV

God said it more than once! Do you hear that? You are IMPORTANT to Him. We are ALL important to Him. He knows everything about us, including the hairs on our heads. God knows us and LOVES us. He cares A LOT! Be encouraged today! Know that you have the Lord God Almighty in your corner! ♡

Have you ever noticed how quickly life can change? A typical scroll through social media shows happy births, unexpected illness and even the grief of death.

In the blink of an eye, our entire lives can change. So what do we do when that happens?

> ""Be still, and know that I am God.""
>
> Psalm 46:10 ESV

> "For we walk by faith, not by sight."
>
> 2 Corinthians 5:7 ESV

> "For nothing will be impossible with God.""
>
> Luke 1:37 ESV

Isn't scripture beautiful? God's word is perfectly written for every need we have. I get excited to see how God will encourage me through scripture. Try it today! Whether life is a struggle or life is going well, go to God's word for direction and encouragement! ♡

Do you have holiday traditions? Maybe you have a specific place where you always gather. Maybe a special menu is always served. Maybe there are always special events like watching afternoon football or even playing a family game.

Regardless of what traditions there may be, what if Jesus showed up as an unexpected guest?

Think about it. Would you swing the door wide open and tell him to come on in and go about the normal events of the day with Jesus by your side? Or would you feel the need to change anything?

Would you suddenly feel like the conversation needed to shift or the music needed to change, or the television needed to be turned off? Would the afternoon festivities be altered? What would you reconsider?

Here is the biggest thought to consider. Jesus isn't an unexpected guest at the door; He is with us every day. Jesus's presence should be our measuring stick for whatever we allow into our lives. Whether it is a big family gathering or just a normal evening at home, would we want Jesus to join our conversations or share a bowl of popcorn while we watch television?

If there is hesitation in our guts, then we may need to consider why. What is in our lives that we wouldn't want to share with Jesus (because He is seeing it anyway)? If we know He wouldn't be part of it, then why are we?

Let's open our doors today and reflect on what Jesus is seeing in our lives. Let's work to live in a way that is more like Jesus. ♡

Do you remember the days of writing essays in school? (Some of you just cringed, didn't you?) Do you remember that we always wrote the rough draft in pencil? Why??? So, we could ERASE!

The same was true in math class. We knew not to solve problems in ink because odds were high that we may need to erase.

Have you ever paused to consider the lines that we have drawn in our Christian lives? You know: the lines we will not cross, the lines that lead us to more sin. How many of us have once said, "I will never..." only to find that we have erased that line over time and now we say, "Well, it isn't so bad." Who changed? God and His Word or us?

> "Do you not know that friendship with the world is enmity with God? Therefore, whoever wishes to be a friend of the world makes himself an enemy of God."
>
> James 4:4 ESV

James was laying it out for folks in chapter four. He is not stepping on toes; he is stomping them. His lessons apply to my life. What about yours? Are you moving the lines of your life boundaries? Go visit this chapter today and see how God may speak to you. ♡

Have you ever planted a garden? Are you a novice or an expert? I have had some successes and failures over the years. One particularly humorous (and aggravating) moment was the one and only time I planted carrots. That little packet held some of the smallest seeds I had ever seen. I raked about 10 feet of my bedded row and proudly scattered those seeds and gently raked back over them. I was so proud until my hubby drove up and began to laugh; he said that little packet of seed would have covered 100 feet rather than my little section. Of course, he was right.

God speaks of seed in His word. This seed is even smaller than those tiny carrot seeds. Read with me.

> He said to them, "Because of your little faith. For truly, I say to you, if you have faith like a grain of mustard seed, you will say to this mountain, 'Move from here to there,' and it will move, and nothing will be impossible for you."
>
> Matthew 17:20

Ouch. Have you ever seen a mustard seed? Google it. It is tiny. Itty bitty. Jesus is speaking to his disciples in this scripture. (I think He is also speaking to you and me.) They had tried to cast a demon out of a young boy and could not. Jesus walked up and immediately freed the boy of this spirit. The disciples were questioning Him about why they were unsuccessful. This was His strong response.

Let me ask. Have you moved any mountains lately? I used to read this scripture and think certainly my faith is bigger than a mustard seed!! Jesus is speaking of PURE, UNDOUBTING, TRUSTFUL; He's GOT this faith. That kind of faith is easier said than done because our world has told us it isn't possible. Our world has told us we are silly to believe.

We MUST practice pushing past these doubts and putting our faith into practice through prayer and trust.

Let's start planting a garden of faith today. ♡

• • •

## Planting Seeds of Faith

Inspiration is like perspiration; it dries up.

How many of us have heard a sermon, attended a youth camp, joined a Bible study, and felt God lighting a fire in our hearts? How many of us have also left that event and found ourselves letting the fire fizzle as we slide right back into our daily routines?

Why is this? Satan doesn't want us on fire for God. He doesn't want us inspired to share God's plan with others. He is standing ready with a fire extinguisher to snuff out whatever God has ignited within us.

Maybe Satan uses doubt ("You can't make this change. You aren't capable of doing this."). Maybe he uses fear (What if you lose friends by taking this stand? What if it impacts your job?).

> "And he said to them, 'Is a lamp brought in to be put under a basket, or under a bed, and not on a stand'?"
>
> Mark 4:21 ESV

> "I press on toward the goal for the prize of the upward call of God in Christ Jesus."
>
> Philippians 3:14 ESV

Our God is greater than this doubt and fear. We just must push through in trust and faith. ♡

Do you know someone personally who has served as a soldier? Has that person ever shared about life as a soldier? I used to love to sit and talk with my grandfather about his time in WWII. Those chats are some of my best reflections with him as I gently tugged on his memories to learn personal bits of history.

Did you know you are also a soldier? As a Christian? We are members of God's army. Look at Paul's words to Timothy in 2 Timothy 2:

> "Share in suffering as a good soldier of Christ Jesus. No soldier gets entangled in civilian pursuits, since his aim is to please the one who enlisted him."
> 2 Timothy 2:3-4 ESV

Did you see that? We are not to lose our focus on Christ. It doesn't say IF we suffer; it says share suffering. KJV says "endure hardness. "So many of us lose faith in Christ because hard times come our way. We tend to think, "God must not love me since He has allowed this to happen." I get it. I have struggled in hardship, too. There are some things I struggle with daily. I am thankful for my faith that grows as I learn more and more about God.

Look at these verses:

> "The saying is trustworthy, for: If we have died with him, we will also live with him; if we endure, we will also reign with him; if we deny him, he also will deny us; if we are faithless, he remains faithful— for he cannot deny himself."
> 2 Timothy 2:11-13 ESV

We are called to be soldiers for God. Are we growing to be good soldiers who stand strong for Him? ♡

Have you ever needed reassurance? Have you ever needed someone to remind you that the truth has been spoken? Have you ever needed reassurance that God's word is real?

There will always be those things that try to cast doubts in our minds, particularly when our minds may want to follow the world. Here are some verses to remind us of all that God's word is forever; His promises have meaning and depth.

> "The grass withers, the flower fades, but the word of our God will stand forever."
>
> Isaiah 40:8 ESV

> "The words of the Lord are pure words, like silver refined in a furnace on the ground, purified seven times."
>
> Psalm 12:6 ESV

> "—and Scripture cannot be broken—"
>
> John 10:35 ESV

> "Heaven and earth will pass away, but my words will not pass away."
>
> Matthew 24:35 ESV

God loves us. God is coming for us. Our salvation is real. Heaven is real. Immerse yourself in scripture today. God's word is like a spring of water that is never-ending. It can refresh even the driest thirst. ♡

# Granny's Fat Dumplings

1 whole chicken (or equivalent chicken parts)
2 cans cream of chicken soup
1-2 tbsp onion powder
Salt and pepper to taste
4 cups all-purpose flour
2 cups warm water

Cook chicken. Remove chicken and debone. Add shredded chicken back to the broth. Set aside on low heat.

Mix flour and water in a large mixing bowl. (Pour one cup of water and begin mixing with the flour. Slowly add the second cup and stop once the flour forms a dough that binds together.) Stir and knead the mixture gently so the dumplings do not become leathery. Turn the heat of the chicken and broth back to med-high.

Sprinkle some flour on the dough ball and on the wax paper or pastry mat. Roll the dough to ¼" thickness. Slice in 1" by 3-4" strips. Drop the dumplings one at a time and stir gently as needed until all are in the pot. Then add the onion powder and cream of chicken soup. Stir gently. Turn the heat to low and allow it to simmer.

● ● ●

Join my daughter, Tyler, and me as we make one of her favorite dishes and reminisce about being spoiled by Granny.

"The same boiling water that softens the potato also hardens the egg. It's about what is inside you, not the circumstances."

Ouch. There is truth in that statement. We have probably all been through some "boiling water" events in our lives. What effect did the events have on our hearts?

Did the challenge draw us to God or away from God? Did our hearts become more open to His love or did we turn to stone?

> "For this people's heart has grown dull, and with their ears they can barely hear, and their eyes they have closed, lest they should see with their eyes and hear with their ears and understand with their heart and turn, and I would heal them.'"
>
> Matthew 13:15 ESV

I have experienced some of both. I'm imperfect, and sometimes I have let events lead to anger or hurt that pulls me away from God. Thankfully, eventually, I take steps back to Him, and He still allows me to be wrapped in His perfect love to begin to heal.

> "The Lord is near to all who call on him, to all who call on him in truth."
>
> Psalm 145:18 ESV

> "Draw near to God, and he will draw near to you."
>
> James 4:8 a ESV

**Life is hard. Choose Jesus.** ♡

A final chat ...Join Pam as she closes this journey with you.

## What does the boiling water of life do to your heart?

Printed in the United States
by Baker & Taylor Publisher Services